BECOMING WOMAN

For Dan

Becoming Woman

The Quest for Wholeness in Female Experience

Penelope Washbourn

Published in San Francisco by
HARPER & ROW, PUBLISHERS
New York, Hagerstown, San Francisco, London

Grateful acknowledgment is made to the following for permission to reprint selections included in this book:

ALFRED A. KNOPF, INC. for excerpts from *The Second Sex* by Simone de Beauvoir, translated and edited by H. M. Parshley. Copyright 1952 by Alfred A. Knopf, Inc. Reprinted by permission of Alfred A. Knopf, Inc.

G. P. PUTNAM'S SONS for excerpts from *Ego and Archetype* by Edward Edinger. Copyright © 1972 by C. G. Jung Foundation for Analytical Psychology.

RANDOM HOUSE INC. for excerpts from *The Nature of Love: Plato to Luther* by Irving Singer. Copyright © 1966 by Irving Singer. Reprinted by permission Random House Inc.

W. W. NORTON AND COMPANY, INC. for excerpts from *Identity, Youth and Crisis* by Erik Erikson. Copyright © 1968 by W. W. Norton and Company Inc. Reprinted by permission of W. W. Norton and Company, Inc.

DR. ALICE GINOTT for quotation from *Between Parent and Child* by Haim G. Ginott. Copyright © 1965 by Haim G. Ginott. Reprinted by permission of Dr. Alice Ginott.

MACMILLAN PUBLISHING COMPANY, INC. for material from *The Golden Bough* (one-volume edition) by Sir James G. Frazer. Copyright 1922 by Macmillan Publishing Co., Inc., Renewed 1950 by Barclays Bank Ltd.

A. P. WATT AND SON for material from *The Golden Bough* (multi-volume edition) by Sir James G. Frazer. By permission of Trinity College Cambridge and the Macmillan Company of London and Basingstoke.

HARPER & ROW, PUBLISHERS, INC. for passages from *The Art of Loving* by Erich Fromm. Copyright 1956 by Erich Fromm. Reprinted by permission of Harper & Row, Publishers, Inc.

FIRST HARPER & ROW PAPERBACK EDITION PUBLISHED 1979.

Designed by Stephanie Krasnow

Library of Congress Cataloging in Publication Data
Washbourn, Penelope.
  Becoming woman.
  Includes bibliographical references and index.
  1. Women. 2. Women—Psychology. 3. Women—Sexual behavior. I. Title.
HQ1206.W27 1976   155.6'33   76-9948
ISBN 0-06-069261-8

81 82 83   10 9 8 7 6 5 4 3

Contents

Preface

A book that is written about the life stages of a woman emerges either from study and observation or from personal experience. In my case, this book has certainly grown from my own personal experience of the stages of life and from my continuing search for a sense of wholeness and integrity.

My personal story begins, as my mother has told me, during a lull in the Blitz. I was born in a hospital in London in 1944, my father being away at the war. I was my parents' third child, the first-born, a boy, having died two weeks after birth. My elder sister was two years older than I and was to exercise considerable influence on me. My parents were educated people from very different backgrounds. My father, the only son of a west country English doctor, was the child of an old father and delicate mother. He represented to me the stability and faded glories of British gentry. My mother, on the other hand, was born in Russia (Estonia) to a Danish engineer and his English wife. When a little girl, her family fled as refugees to Britain during the Russian revolution. From her I derived a sense of the need for strength to survive in the face of the transience of life and also her aesthetic sensibilities. From my father and his love of the English countryside in which he grew up, I derived a

simple sense of the beauty of nature, a love of the outdoors and
the goodness of life.

My father's new career after the war took him from his re-
search in the Natural Science Museum into a government post
abroad to develop cultural links between the two countries. His
job with the British Council moved us from Belgium in 1947 to
Sweden in 1948, and to Finland from 1949 to 1953. Two other
children were born after me. My earliest memories of Belgium
were of my nursery school, where I spoke French, and the
playground on the roof that frightened me because of the black
tar and the nooks and crannies in which one could hide. In
Sweden I played with Swedish children and began to speak
Swedish. It was on my fifth birthday in Finland, sitting on the
woodbox in the kitchen that I came to my first existential self-
realization that I was I, a totally separate person, Penny, and
this was *my* day. The years in Finland are full of memories of
pleasure and pain and the fears of negotiating my existence in a
foreign land. There was the terrible feeling of being in a Swedish–speaking school where nobody spoke English apart from one
teacher, of hating the meat soup at school and being forced to
eat it, of walking to school in the morning in the winter while it
was still dark, of sucking on icicles. Then there was the time of
playing truant with my friend and running away from home, of
going to stay with a friend at the summer cottage and being
dared to walk past the tree where there was an adder's nest, of
learning to row and to swim.

There are also early memories of religion. The Anglican
church for expatriates was held in an apartment that had been
converted into a small chapel. The lobby and church were always full of the smell of burning toast from the flat next door.
The Book of Common Prayer was introduced to me with a
distinctive aroma. I found these early Sunday observances very
boring. Rather more fun was the playacting of Old Testament
stories in the Sunday school. I enjoyed the role of Potiphar's
wife. Anglicanism at this point laid no great hold on my childish
imagination.

The golden, onion-domed Russian Orthodox church stood

menacing and imposing near our apartment building. We used to play around it and get shouted at by an angry old lady in a language we could not understand. On Good Friday when I was eight we went inside for the first time. The church was huge and dark, filled with people holding flickering candles and with glimpses of gold around the icons. Everyone was standing and the candles were guttering, spilling wax onto the floor. In the middle was a huge bier covered with flowers. There was a choir singing unaccompanied some of the most beautiful and sad music I had ever heard. The priests were all dressed up in splendid robes and were somewhat hidden from us by a screen. People went one by one to kiss the flowers which covered the body of Jesus. I went too, knelt and kissed the flowers. The incredible beauty and sadness of that Good Friday service, all in a language I could not understand, touched me more deeply than any prayerbook service of burnt toast expatriate Anglicanism could ever do. My journey into liturgy and sacramental religion was about to begin.

The return of the family to England in my ninth year was the beginning of a new stage. Schooled for the first time in an English system, I struggled with learning new weights and measures and in expressing myself in English. My father underwent a shift in religious affiliation and the family (apart from my older sister who was away at boarding school) began attendance at an Anglo-Catholic church. I loved it. Sunday school, Mass and eventually Confirmation, going to confessions, observing Lent, became the focus of my life in my early adolescent years. The church was friendly, the "Father" was outgoing and loving, and the ritual filled my senses with joy. Music, color, song, the dramatic action of the liturgy, the sadness and joy of the church's calendar, the silence and mystery of those services, gave me great pleasure. I was excellent at being holy and earning all the religious pictures for Sunday school attendance. I went most often with my father and sensed his strong attachment to this new religious framework. We talked religion to and from church.

Another important influence at this time was the intense

rivalry with my elder sister. I felt I was "bullied" by her and used to complain loudly to my parents. She was smarter, physically stronger and in every way dominated me. I hated her. My drive to succeed emerged subconsciously, I now believe, to *show* her, to *show* my parents that I could do as well as she. Oh, how I hated her. The only area she had no interest in, —indeed she boldly proclaimed at the age of 13 that she was an atheist,—was the field of religion. She scorned going to church, whereas I, as I now see, got close to my father through being religious. She had his attention at all other levels, but the religious domain was mine.

My academic career was always a surprise to me. After the initial difficulties of adjusting to the new system, I struggled with math and English, and found gradual competence in languages, history and of course, religion. My sister's academic brilliance foreshadowing me by two years led me to undervalue my own competence. I thought of myself in my early teens as a "people" person, whereas *she* was of course "the clever" one. And yet I suppose I got along with her also. She shared "the facts" of life with me when I was about ten and we enjoyed the same sense of humor. We were unhappily not trusted friends in adolescence, but suffered alone the sexual yearnings of pubescent girls in blue serge uniforms for the boys we passed on the street. My lack of romance until the age of 18 was the occasion of deep frustration to me. Educated in a girls' school of high quality, I gradually experienced a sense of my growing intellectual ability. Having gone through the fantasies of "being a probation officer," "working with children" and, of course, "becoming a nun," I began to have a more realistic picture of my own capabilities. Dedicated women school teachers who saw strength and encouraged it provided me with a sense of possible goals beyond my highest dreams, the university degree. I chose the field of religion over that of history because I felt that there was no other area of study that was so intensely stimulating both intellectually and personally. I felt that theology *mattered*, that there was an existential basis for the discussion of religion. I felt that I could be subjectively involved in this area of study as I could in no other. In that perception I have never been disappointed.

The end of my high school career also marked the end of my personal piety. Gone were the aesthetic delights of ritual. In its place I began to see dogmatism, narrowness and a lack of intellectual integrity. The end of my faith as a child began as my study of religion progressed. The more I knew, the less I believed. This conflict continued throughout university. I felt guilty: an unbelieving theologian! My university experience was a growth to a new sense of autonomy. Growing in intellectual strengths I found that I was also for the first time aware of my own sexuality. My conflict existed in finding a relation between the two. As a woman in the field of religion, I was considered on oddity by men. "What are you going to be, a nun?," they used to joke. To my colleagues in theology I was an intellectual threat and they ignored my female body hidden by my black gown. The dichotomy between the mind and body was strong. My male professors encouraged and responded to my enthusiasm for my theological studies. In my social life when first introduced to a man I would lie and say I was in Philosophy, rather than deal with the negative implications of being a "religious" woman.

My experiences at the university began another transition from my British middle class environment to a broader one. Disobeying university policy, three fellow women students and I moved from campus to the slums of Nottingham and set up residence in a flat above a fish-and-chip shop. The reality of poverty, racism, alcoholism and the impact of industrialization in inner core areas of midland British towns began to erode my middle-class complacency. Living within that social environment with the blackened lace factories still dominating the landscape changed my view of religion. For the first time I saw that religion must be socially relevant, that it should "make a difference" to the quality of life.

The experience of living in the slums provided me also with a new view of cooperative living. Sharing all expenses and tasks we lived on a minimum income and yet we had everything in the

world. The collegiality and sense of community and sharing
made those days above the fish-and-chip shop a joy and a model
for a new way of living. My commitment to "socialism" both
intellectually and as a mode of living was being experienced at
first hand.

The transition to the slums of Nottingham marked the beginning of my association with those who had wider visions than
England, i.e. the United States. My initial trip was an adventure
into a new world. I remembered setting off alone by Greyhound
bus and the day I arrived in New York. I spent the major part
of the summer as a camp counselor in Vermont and found new
friends who invited me to visit their homes.

On returning to England I wrestled with my future. What was
I to do with my theology? My options were limited: teach religion in high school, go into social work, or continue my studies.
The Church of England I had long dismissed. There was no
vocational place for me there as a woman. Being at this stage
dissatisfied with the smugness and intellectual narrowness of
British theology, I applied to come to the United States for one
year's study. My professor had contact with Union Theological
Seminary in New York City and encouraged me to apply there.
Receiving a fellowship for one year's study at Union was my
entree to a new country, a new intellectual environment, a new
stage in my life. I felt that in the United States theology would
be "relevant" to the social problems of the world, that it was
not a closed discipline. In that premonition I was not to be
mistaken.

I lived in New York from 1965–1971, in which time there
was the Columbia University student "revolt," the Vietnam
draft issue, and the assassinations of Bobby Kennedy and Martin
Luther King. My theology was shaped not only by the people
I studied—Paul Tillich and Alfred North Whitehead and
the process theologians—but also by the social context in
which I lived. My colleagues were going to jail for burning their
draft cards, the seminary president's wife was involved in
demonstrations. Reinhold Niebuhr came to preach on the immorality of the Vietnam War, and the sirens screeched on

Broadway as they raced towards Harlem during those long, hot summers when other cities were burning in the ghettoes. I was mugged outside my own apartment building and lived with fear as I walked home from the subway at night.

My sense of the "tragic" dimension of life, the ambiguity of human existence and yet the grace that transcended that darkness, was enhanced by living in the community of Union in the center of New York. I loved and hated that city. It was intense, intellectually stimulating, dehumanizing, and wonderful. All races, all languages, beliefs and tastes were there. Every human problem that urban life would experience was to be found in New York. I lived through the blackout, the garbage strike, the subway strike, the newspaper strike. New York terrified me and yet it was a community in which I felt alive and free to be whatever I wanted to be.

My introduction to process theology and my choice to continue studying for my Ph.D. in this area was the intellectual framework for truths that I knew from experience. Life is dynamic, ongoing, creative and destructive. Life is organically interconnected, a society of individuals in communion with one another. God is not outside the universe but immanent within it. My childhood sacramentalism was finding new expression in a theology which fitted my own outlook on life and enabled me to integrate my intellectual framework with my personal perceptions. I began to understand the meaning of a resurrection faith on an entirely new level. The memorial service to Martin Luther King symbolized that new reality. Out of the depths of the community's despair came hope, black and white joined in confession and praise, and I felt the presence of a strength among us in that worship which moved me to tears.

On a personal level my womanhood was still left far behind. The dichotomy between mind and body persisted, except now I was living in an exclusively theological community. I felt they did not 'see' me as a woman. I suffered loneliness as well as the shock of adjusting to a new culture. I was beginning to fear that being a woman in the field of religion was destroying my chances of normal relationships with men.

Then I met a musician, a foreign student who worked in the church where I led youth groups. Our relationship developed slowly. Through him I was introduced to a whole world of New York music which enthralled me. We did not talk about my philosophy and theology, nor could I understand the intricacies of his music, but we appreciated each other's sexuality and so nine months after we had met, we became lovers. After a month he was gone, off to a summer job and then to a new career and I spent the following year writing letters, paying visits to Indiana, and being alone. We supported each other from afar in our mutual loneliness. His decision to return to New York the following year for study precipitated our plans for marriage. I planned the wedding and he arrived the week before. The reality of the marriage was not what I had expected. Incapable of finding a level of communication and trust we each suffered in silence. By the second year my pain took me to counselling and to a decision to ask for separation.

I began to explore in therapy my own sense of failure. My woman Jungian therapist pointed me in a direction that religion and theology had never suggested: the uniqueness of my female identity and the spiritual value of my own self as a continuous journey in life, through many modes of self-expression and encounter. With these dim glimmers of a beginning self-awareness, I began a new relationship, where love and passion and conflict were all mixed together.

This last year in New York was also the beginning of my awareness of the need to integrate my female sexuality with my theological studies. There were other women who were searching for new models for theological expression using their female experience. My first essay on the possibility of a feminine theology (1971) began this process of personal reintegration of head and body that continues to this day. This essay, my first publication five years ago, also began the association with my editor and publisher, leading finally to this book.

My life faced another crisis. My new love accepted a position in Canada. Our relationship was quite unclear in terms of future commitment. I knew I could not go with him. The relationship seemed over. I took a teaching position in a small town in Ohio and there experienced culture shock once again. New York had been my norm for America! Rural Ohio was quite different. While successful at my teaching I experienced a sense of isolation among my male colleagues. There was no place for socializing with a single separated woman. It was a difficult year. I was isolated from all friends, and the smallness of the town was deadening. I gained strength from learning to drive.

Risking all, I flew to Canada to clarify the possibility of a future for our relationship. The relationship developed again over the distance as we journeyed back and forth and ran up huge phone bills. The commitment to marry led to a search for jobs in the same place and when I was offered one in Canada, I moved to Winnipeg. Going to Santo Domingo to get the divorce had been an experience of strength for me, yet moving once again to a new country, a new culture, a new job and a new marriage and my first pregnancy were very hard. After four years in Canada I am beginning to find a new sense of my identity as a woman, as a theologian, as a wife and as a parent. The experience of carrying our first child and of giving birth so easily and quickly by "natural childbirth" provided me with the material and the need to integrate that aspect of my sexuality with my search for a religious dimension of spirituality. This book was born during the latter months of my second pregnancy in the summer of 1975. As my baby grew inside, so the pages fell from my pen. The creative process was both biological and literary.

I realize now that my recent writing in the area of religion and female sexuality, including this book, does not represent a total departure from the intellectual or religious heritage in which I was nourished, either in England or in New York. The attempt to write of the spiritual dimensions of the female life cycle has only become an issue to me as I have recently realized that theology springs not only from the head but from the heart. In learning to accept my own particular joys and sorrows as valuable resources for spiritual insight, I have discovered the validity of being a woman in the field of religion. Perhaps the transitional character of my life, the many stages and crises I have had, is somewhat unique, but I experience them still as I now struggle to come to terms with myself as a parent and to continue to grow in my marriage. Trusting in the ongoingness of life, finding grace and joy in its gifts of strength and wonder means to me accepting the pains and vulnerabilities so clearly visible in the preceding paragraphs. I am still beginning in that journey of self-trust.

Introduction

My conviction is that religious questions and reflections about the meaning of what is holy or ultimate arise at times of crisis in the life of the individual and of the community. These crises may be historical or personal events, but because of them we are forced to respond to a new situation. The question of the meaning of our identity and our attitude toward life is challenged. A crisis is a time of change, anxiety, and possibility. Something new happens, and we summon resources from the past, as well as discover new strengths, to deal with the implications of our changed situation.

Psychologists since the time of Sigmund Freud have described human development in terms of *life-crises* or stages of personal growth. From the viewpoint of psychology one must more or less "successfully" negotiate each stage in order to advance to the next. Erik Erikson views these crises, particularly those from adolescence onward, as involving questions of a religious nature, for the individual's identity must be renegotiated in terms of a new understanding of the meaning and purpose of the whole.[1]

For a woman, the most significant life-crises are associated with having a female body. Most psychological literature writes of the "stages of man" or "man's search for meaning" and to a large extent ignores the distinctive aspect of the female life-crises. I propose that a woman's search for psychological and spiritual wholeness goes through the particular life-crises of being a female body. These stages are not just psychological phases to be negotiated but turning points that raise fundamentally religious questions. At each juncture a woman must redefine her self-identity in relation to her perception of the purpose of life and in relation to her understanding of her own identity in relation to that ultimate value.

Traditional religious rituals in many societies are associated with these life-crises. In primitive societies as well as in industrialized cultures we humans have needed to construct rituals around the significant events in the life of a woman and her relation to the community. The birth of a child, the advent of puberty, growth into adulthood, marriage rites, and funeral rites exemplify our need to signify or make meaning out of the major events that mark our lives. Even in our secular society we have versions of religious rituals to symbolize our passage through life: graduation from high school, the stag party before the wedding, the retirement dinner, the golden anniversary, and the funeral service. These events are personal and communal. They mark significant changes in the life of the individual and the community. Richard Rubenstein in his book *After Auschwitz* suggested that ritual arises out of the need of the individual in community to give meaning to the questions of personal or social identity. Ritual expresses our search for a new identity in relation to the past and to the future and thus emerges from the life-crises—events that force us to deal with questions of self-identity in relation to ultimate value.[2]

Building upon Erikson's understanding of the life-crises and Rubenstein's view of the necessity for "rites of passage" to mark those events, I propose to explore the life-crises of being a woman and the personal and spiritual questions implicit within those crises. The image of the new woman that is emerging from the contemporary discussion on the role of women in society has yet to deal significantly with the search for personal wholeness that includes the implications of being a female body. Women's new search for self-understanding implies an integration of the unique female body structure into a continuing personal quest. I believe that in and through the life-crises the questions of personal meaning are most radically presented to woman today. They force her to choose what she will become, what type of identity she will have, and how she will interpret her femaleness in relation to the whole. The crisis opens an option for personal growth and also offers the possibility for a most destructive form of self-interpretation of femaleness and its relation to others. I call these options the *graceful* and the *demonic* possibilities. At each stage of life it is possible for a woman to understand and interpret the dimensions of her identity as graceful or demonic. To perceive female sexuality gracefully involves seeing it within the process of becoming more fully human and with an understanding of the purpose of life. To interpret female sexuality demonically means to find a false sense of identity in the female role—to romanticize it, to manipulate it, or to see it as an end in itself. The ability to perceive the graceful dimensions of female sexuality will depend largely upon a woman's ability to express the questions of meaning raised by her life-crises within a community context. Women *need* "rites of passage" that symbolize the hopes, fears, and questions of ultimate meaning in their search for personal and social identity in contemporary society.

This book will discuss these major personal events from the perspective of the woman. Some of these crises are shared by men but raised in a particular manner, and from an essentially female perspective, the problem of personal identity, the nature of ultimate meaning, and the structure of the relation between the individual and society.

1.

Menstruation

One day I woke up and my bed was a sea of blood. I felt so ashamed and told my mother. She took me to the bathroom and I was shown the belt and pads and how to use them. My mother told me to keep myself clean, change the pads often and wash out my pants if they got stained. I was told that now I was a woman and could get pregnant. I wasn't too sure I enjoyed the status of being a woman, but rather hated the restrictions that having my period placed on going swimming with the boys and doing Phys. ed. at school. All of a sudden I was different. I hated the odor that came with wearing the pads, their bulkiness and fearing that they might show or leak through. I was so embarrassed at home when I had to dispose of the pads in case anyone should notice. Then there was the discomfort: it was real and the blood used to flow and flow, for days on end it seemed. I suppose I felt proud I had finally started since mother had told me about it some years before. (I remember how embarrassed she was!) and then other girls at school had started. We used to call it the "curse" in our house and so it was for me. It was several years before a friend told me you could have a bath during your period. In later years one of the best side effects of being on the pill was that it lessened the flow dramatically.

The first major crisis in the life of a woman is the onset of menstruation. It shocks her radically. One day she is a child; the next she is a new reality, part of an ongoing process of life that inevitably conditions her self-understanding but whose purpose and nature she is as yet unable to comprehend. Menstruation creates anxiety, not only or particularly because of the physical discomfort or the lack of information about it, but because it implies the need for a new self-understanding based on a new body experience. Simone de Beauvoir wrote forcibly of the re-actions of a girl to menstruation in terms of being trapped. "The set fate that up to now weighed upon her indistinctly and from without is crouching in her belly; there is no escape; she feels she is caught."[1]

It appears that for women in our own society the experience of menstruation is still ambiguous, not merely because of lack of information or old-fashioned methods of absorbing the blood. Our method of handling menstruation today is to ap-proach it primarily on the physiological level. We give girls information about the reproductive organs and the names and the functions of the ova, the endometrium, the uterus, and the pituitary gland. We also give them pamphlets printed in pink entitled *The Miracle of You: What It Means to Be a Girl*[2] which not only relay technical information but also present a thoroughly enthusiastic view of the changes inherent in men-struation.

Menstruation and all the other interesting and exciting physical changes that gradually take place as you grow up indicate that nature is gently and gradually preparing your body and mind for your most likely future role, that of a mother. . . . Since menstrua-tion makes motherhood possible you should think of it as a good and healthy bodily function. . . . So you see that to be a girl is very special. It means that the most protective, life-giving role in the world is yours. No wonder that nature, with great and loving care, begins to equip you to function as a woman as you approach your teens.[3]

The problem with this approach is that it tends to ignore that anxiety created by menstruation is not only caused by a lack of knowledge concerning the processes or function of the female body structure but by the fact that menstruation is a crisis in self-identity. It is a dramatic event in the life of a girl who is full of hopes and real fears. It signifies the end of one life and the beginning of another whose character is as yet undisclosed. In menstruation a female's body is taken over by what is experienced as a sudden force, determining, controlling, and affecting life from now on. The psychologist Judith Bardwick suggested that our culture's very denial of the crisis character of menstruation *increases* a woman's anxiety about it.[4] A recent study on attitudes toward menstruation suggested that the greater the emphasis on the traditional motherhood roles, the greater the physical and emotional distress experienced at menstruation by a young woman.[5]

The experience of menstruation for the young girl as associated with shame, guilt, and fear is perceived by many psychologists as part of a learned response affected by parental and cultural conditioning and the persistence of traditional religious taboos. Germaine Greer suggested that "what we ought to see in the agonies of puberty is the result of the conditioning that maims the female personality in creating the feminine."[6] However, I feel that menstruation is experienced as anxiety by the young girl, not only because of cultural attitudes toward the female body or because of the personality type of the girl involved,[7] but because menstruation is essentially a dramatic physical and emotional event. It is physically dramatic because it involves a flow of blood that must be dealt with, not just in terms of sanitary procedures, but in terms of psychological implications. It is emotionally dramatic because one day it begins and will continue until menopause. Though the body has been preparing for that day for many years, for the young girl *that* day marks the end of childhood and the beginning of adulthood. In the life of a man the developments of puberty are more gradual. Erich Neumann suggested that menstruation is of far greater significance to the woman than the first emission of semen is to the man. A man very often cannot remember when emission first occured, whereas menstruation for the woman marks a radical change which is never insignificant.[8]

The ambiguity of menstruation is also due to the fact that it involves a bloodlike discharge. Karen Paige's studies suggested that the anxiety associated with menstruation varies with the amount of blood, not with the hormone levels of the woman.[9] In most cultures blood is regarded as "life-blood," to be preserved and not spilled. To give blood is to give someone else life. In menstruation nature sheds blood in a manner contradictory to all usual understandings of the loss of blood. Here bleeding is a cleansing, the very opposite of other kinds of bleeding. While we may understand this rationally, on the emotional level this blood flow appears to violate our sense of what is normal. Perhaps our modern culture's failure to appreciate the ambiguity of menstruation causes many young girls to experience it in loneliness and with anxiety. We fail to see that it raises some fundamental and troubling questions about the meaning of a girl's identity. She is linked with the processes of nature in a manner that may be glorious in its outcome but initially is at best a nuisance. In our culture where marriage and childbirth are so delayed, perhaps ten or fifteen years beyond the onset of menstruation, it is hard for the ten-year-old girl to appreciate that she is now a biologically mature female. With menstruation comes the possibility of pregnancy; yet that too is seen immediately as a liability rather than a potential joy. In North American society fertility is devalued, and we prescribe for it certain limited means of expression. The young girl knows that she is now a sexual being, but the reality of her body and her emotional and social being are out of joint. She is a woman in body and still a child in spirit or in social standing. Her family and the community regard the potential of her body with suspicion since the fertility of young girls is a cause for anxiety rather than celebration. It is hard for us in this society to find a way of celebrating. In our rational framework we tend to ignore the experience of menstruation for the young girl as a major crisis which demands the formulation of a new identity and self-image.

Primitive cultures understand that the onset of menstruation is a special event that needs a ritual to mark it, a "rite of passage." This perception is not necessarily caused by a lack of understanding the female physiology but emerges from a wiser sense that the beginning of menstruation involves a qualitative change in a girl's being.[10] This change offers a possibility, both for the individual and for the community, of being a blessing or a curse. Menstruation symbolizes the advent of a new power that is *mana* or "sacred." A sacred power has life-giving and life-destroying possibilities, and in no case is *mana* to be taken lightly. A *taboo* expresses this feeling that something special, some holy power, is involved, and our response to it must be very careful. Even those societies which appear to have only negative attitudes toward menstruation, that is, place many restrictive taboos on the menstruating female and the community, are expressing a deep understanding of the essential sacredness of the event and of the need to insure the beneficial effects of this sacred power.

In primitive cultures the onset of menstruation is an ambiguous experience to be celebrated as well as feared. This explains why the rituals appear to fall into two categories, a cause for dancing and a cause for seclusion of the girl. In either case the ritual marks an understanding that the girl needs a symbolic, interpretive framework as she negotiates her first life-crisis and redefines herself as a mature female. These rituals also express an understanding that discovering our identity as women is not to be a solitary struggle but is to be worked out within the context of the community. In each primitive ritual a form of self-transformation is expressed through trials, symbolic acts, and words which promote healing and integrate the forces at play. The girls and the community move into a new identity *through* the crisis.

White Painted Woman spoke to the people and said: 'When the girls first menstruate you shall have a feast. Let there be songs and dancing for the girls for four nights. Let the Gahe dance in the east in front of the ceremony." Today masked dancers personify the Gahe in the rite. The girl herself must not sleep for the four days and nights; on the fifth morning she must make four runs around the ritual baskets, while the woman who has care of her during the rite chants the shrill praisecall and prays for her. The songs are sacred prayer songs, among them homeopathic songs to White Painted Woman.

> White Painted Woman carries this girl,
> She carries her through long life,
> . . . to good fortune,
> . . . to old age,
> She bears her to peaceful sleep.

On the morning of the fifth day, while the girl runs into the sunrise, the last song is sung beginning with the moving words: "You have started out on the good earth."[11]

Even in those cultures where rituals appear most cruel and restrictive, there is an understanding that the sacred power involved is an enormous potential for good or for evil and that a form of initiation or integration of this new reality is necessary. At the end of the seclusion a new being emerges. One such typical rite documented by Sir James Frazer expresses this concept of transformation:

Amongst the Tlingit (Thlinkeet) of Kolosh Indians of Alaska, when a girl showed signs of womanhood she used to be confined to a little hut or cage, which was completely blocked up with the exception of a small air-hole. In this dark and filthy abode she had to remain a year, without fire, exercise or associates. Only her mother and a female slave might supply her with nourishment. Her food was put in at the little window; she had to drink out of the wing-bone of a white-headed eagle. The time of her seclusion was afterwards reduced in some places to six or three months or even less. She had to wear a sort of hat with long flaps, that her gaze might not pollute the sky; for she was thought unfit for the sun to shine upon and it was imagined that her look would destroy the luck of a hunter, fisher or gambler, turn things to stone, and do other mischief. At the end of her confinement her old clothes were burnt, new ones were made, and a feast was given, at which a slit was cut in her upper lip parallel to the mouth, and a piece of wood or shell was inserted to keep the aperture open.[12]

It is important to locate in ourselves the psychological and emotional roots of these primitive rituals. In their lack of understanding or superstition, prescientific cultures nevertheless have an innate wisdom concerning the implications of the onset of menstruation. It is seen as a life-crisis, a time when the individual and the group need to express their awareness of the radical significance of the event. Even where the stress is on secluding the girl[13] and the potential polluting effect of menstrual blood,[14] it is evident that menstruation is viewed as the supernatural strength of the woman, and the concern is for the sacred power of the menstrual blood. The response of men in certain Australian tribes is to try to imitate this creative power by slitting the penis[15] to make an artificial vulva.

Another element of menstruation taboos that is frequently ignored is the real need of the girl to withdraw psychologically and physically into solitude or into the presence of other women. This dramatic event brings a need for introspection, aloneness, and recontacting inner depths.[16] A girl must wrestle with the meaning of her female identity, and withdrawal may have a positive function. Erich Neumann goes so far as to suggest that all taboos originated in the menstruation taboos which were *imposed by* women on themselves and on men. Monthly segregation was a movement of women into a sacred female precinct which focused around the life-giving power of the woman.[17]

The idea that ritual and taboos involve a positive as well as a negative element corresponds to my suggestion that the onset of menstruation is a time of danger, a *crisis*. The resolution is unclear at the outset; it may be creative or destructive. Our culture has ignored the crisis character of menstruation and so is unable to provide young women with a framework within which the mystery, that is, the joyful and fearful elements, may be expressed and integrated into a new form of self-understanding. I agree with Esther Harding's statement that the rationalization of the sacred aspect of menstruation in our culture has resulted in a psychological loss for women.[18] Technical information will not answer the fundamental questions.

All myths and rites arise at moments of psychological danger. "They magically conjure forth the life energies of the individual and his group to meet and surpass the dangers."[19] For the woman today menstruation involves danger in terms of the choices she must make concerning her new self-understanding as a sexually mature female. She may be overwhelmed by the frightening and fearful elements of the experience and internalize an understanding of her body as something to be mistrusted and to be ashamed of. Unfortunately it is particularly hard for a woman in this culture to avoid two contradictory and finally psychologically limiting possibilities: she either identifies her new self with her body in its negative or positive aspects, or she tries to ignore the body completely by adopting a business-as-usual attitude toward it.

In this first life-crisis the young woman makes decisions, usually on an unconscious level, about an attitude toward her female identity as a sexual body and its relation to her self-image and her sense of purpose in life and the relation of her body to the world at large, particularly to men. The danger involved is that she may be unable to integrate the crisis into the formation of her continuing personal maturation which proceeds in and through the experiences of her female body but which is not identical with any one of them. This is a *spiritual* crisis because the issue at stake is not just a personal question but involves redefining the self in context of the purpose of nature, understanding one's physicality in relation to the pro-creativity of nature, and deciding about one's goal and purpose in life in human community. To answer the questions, Who am I? What does this mean for my life? one must come to terms with several other questions: What does it all mean? What relation does my female sexuality have to that purpose of the whole? Is that purpose creative or destructive? Is there any point to it or is my particular physiology irrelevant to questions of ultimate meaning?

The ability of a young woman to "successfully" negotiate the life-crisis of menstruation depends first on a recognition of it as a crisis by the girl and by the community. Ignoring its importance leaves the individual to struggle alone with her feelings and fears and provides no means for their expression. *Recognizing* does not necessarily imply *discussing* or providing information although facts about menstruation are important as a preparation for the actual onset. *Recognizing* means marking the occasion so that the girl is supplied a symbolic framework within which to find resources for her questions of meaning. To ignore the event means that the girl's new framework will be casually formed by fears and rumors and by what the culture of school and society teach her about the nature of her identity as a woman. Cultural attitudes conveyed through media, advertising, and common role expectations do not, however, creatively answer her question of female identity. Instead she concludes that her body is valued as second rate, and she learns she must become, as Germaine Greer has suggested, a "female eunuch."

The resolution of the crisis of menstruation may be called *demonic* when it is not only destructive for the ongoing life of the woman but actively produces ill effects in the lives of others. A demonic resolution fails to understand the relation between the quest for personal identity and having a female body with its sexual structure; female sexuality is a positive part of that quest rather than outside it or restricting it. The first most common destructive solution to the crisis of menstruation is being overcome by fear, shame, and guilt and internalizing any negative parental or social attitudes. When this happens, a girl learns to experience her body primarily as dirty and disgusting.

A woman told me a story about her first period. Soon after she began to menstruate she had left visible signs of blood in the toilet bowl. Her father saw it and scolded her, warning her never to let her brother see any of those "digusting things." Her shame and embarrassment were complete. Since that time she has always checked the bathroom and toilet bowl feverishly to make sure she has left no sign of that dreaded "curse." This woman is now in her twenties and has a great deal of difficulty in finding positive value in her own female sexuality.

To experience the onset of menstruation as predominantly frightening rather than positive is, in my experience, fairly com-

mon for women in this society. This is partly because of the
necessary ambiguity of the phenomenon, but it is also because
the positive element is so difficult to articulate or locate in our
framework. Menstruation is messy and inconvenient with emotional and physical discomforts, even in these days of tampons
and pain remedies. We do not like to be inconvenienced. The
image of humanness that predominates our industrialized society is based on the mind controlling the body. To be limited by
our bodies, whether in sickness or death, or particularly by the
female body processes, is considered weakness and threatens
our "normal" forms of mastery and self-control. We try to overcome fatigue or pain with drugs and stimulants and fail to accept our bodies as part of an ongoing life-process which has its
own rhythms. To regard menstruation primarily as an unfortunate nuisance that now can be handled largely through better
sanitary products is to treat female sexuality as an unfortunate
burden or weakness which can to a large extent be overcome
and thus ignored. This solution is very prevalent in our society,
and it implies an inability to integrate the female body structure
into the process of identity formation. This lack of self-acceptance and trust of the body stems from being unable to experience any value in female sexuality.

Another limiting interpretation of sexuality may be to identify oneself with it entirely. The traditional identification of the
female with the role of mother may have provided previous
generations with a sense of purpose and an identity in relation
to the whole. Even in primitive societies the quest for personal
wholeness is linked with an understanding of the ongoing procreative life-process. In that sense, the onset of menstruation as
the symbol of one's role within the ultimate purpose of the
universe was not *demonic* but *graceful*. Fertility is seen, not as a
woman's personal power, but as the power of the fertility goddess in whose power all humans and animals participated and in
relation to whom women can perceive their sexuality as a gift
and a medium whereby the transcendent life-giving power of
nature expresses itself.

This option is no longer open to women, for many years

stretch between puberty and marriage, and women's life-span extends beyond childbearing years. Also neither men nor women see their whole identity bound up with imitating the procreative power of nature. Our understanding of the creative purpose of life does include procreativity, but it is not identified with it or limited by it. Our understanding of fertility is also very different. We do not value persons *because* of their pro-creative potential; indeed, unrestricted numbers of children are now seen as destructive of the whole rather than creative.

The solution to the crisis of menstruation for a young woman in our society is not *gracefully* answered by the sole response, motherhood. To opt for motherhood in solution to the quest for personal identity in relation to ultimate meaning is to opt for a *demonic* rather than *graceful* solution. It is self-deceptive to perceive female procreative power as a personal right and a source of ego gratification and not in relation to a cosmic purpose. It is demonic in the sense that identity and fertility are not synonymous either in terms of the years of a woman's life or in terms of the creative potential of human life that includes but is not restricted to procreativity. To answer the questions of personal identity raised by menstruation by "motherhood" is confusing in that it creates greater anxiety for the young girl in her teenage years. Her sexuality is interpreted as aimed solely toward finding a mate but at the same time is geared toward protecting her virginity. However, "irresponsible" pregnancies are not welcomed in this society. Pregnancy is only legitimate within certain defined limits. To answer "motherhood" is demonic, for it demands that a young girl find her identity in one biological role which finally restricts the integration of her sexuality into a mature relationship with a male. The problems caused for the woman by resolving this early life-crisis in this manner are evident in our society, not only in the restrictive and possessive attitudes evident in mothers toward their children, but also in the destructive effects for potential resolution of future life-crises in the individual woman. To glorify, senti-mentalize, and totally identify personal meaning with the fertile potential of the female body structure is a delusion, for it fails to recognize the ambiguity implicit within the experience of menstruation.

Another negative solution to the onset of menstruation would be to fail to take it seriously. This response can lead to an attitude that fails to integrate what is happening to the body with personal selfhood. Lack of self-awareness and responsibility may be a means of protecting ourselves from the recognition of a force that affects our being and that has creative and destructive potential. In not wishing to acknowledge the "fateful" quality of this reality, the young girl and her society can fail to provide a framework within which the nature of the event can be expressed. To ignore it does not mean that the young girl has succeeded in integrating the experience into her self-understanding. It can lead to later attitudes toward her body and its expression in relation to others that lack responsibility and are unconsciously manipulative. The impersonality of menstruation needs to be integrated into *personal* self-understanding in order for the next life-crisis, a girl's expression of sexuality in relation to others, to be defined creatively.

The *graceful* experience of menstruation would be to accept it as a symbol of the potential of one's body for the enrichment of self and others. To emphasize that the life-power and process made evident in your body every month is pleasure-giving does not mean to underestimate the negativity and anxiety associated with the onset of menstruation. Menstruation is an ending as well as a beginning, and the ability to experience the new potential opened up by it depends on being able to wrestle with the fears associated with being biologically female. We must express the fears of our "being determined," the divisions between women and men made evident by it, and the anxieties concerned with our potential fertility. The graceful acceptance of menstruation is possible only through recognizing its ambiguous quality; it does not imply a simplistic attitude toward the body. Nature is cruel as well as kind, and life proceeds through loss. Our creative potential as individuals depends at all levels on giving up something, letting go some aspects of ourselves. At menstruation, childhood is no more; that freedom, innocence, and simplicity is gone forever.

To emerge gracefully from the life-crisis of menstruation would imply in our society that we are able to celebrate the value of our female body structure as potentially childbearing without identifying ourselves with it. As young girls we need to be able to participate imaginatively in that possibility offered by being female and to know that it is a good that we may be able, if we are fortunate and if we choose, to experience. The onset of menstruation can symbolize the power of our bodies to give us joy, deepen and enrich our experience of life, and increase the totality of our self-expression. The potential procreativity of our bodies is not a personal power but the linking of ourselves to the creative power of nature and to the creative aspect of all human relationships.

Do you remember that time when your period was a source of joy? There was that dreaded time when you feared you were pregnant. Every day you checked to see if there was even a hint of color. Not a sign. Anxiously waiting, will it never come? And then that day when the flow returned—the relief, the blessed relief! Floodgates open, pour down blessed tide: never have menstrual flows been more welcome, more graceful!

To celebrate the particular potential of the female sexual structure does not imply identifying one's goal in life with the power of fertility. It means rather understanding that our bodies are to be owned as good. They are of high value for ourselves and for creating good for others, but they are not the totality of our identity. The potential for childbearing may be expressed at some distant point in the future and then only a few times, if at all. Childbearing is not an ultimate good, the beginning and end of a woman's identity. It does offer a new opportunity in the life of a young girl, a sexual structure whose possible utilization for pregnancy and birth bears a particularly valuable potential. In this context we may celebrate the goodness of life as we experience it in and through our bodies.

To emerge enriched from the life-crisis of menstruation implies finally trusting and liking one's body. Trusting it means being peaceful with it, knowing its potential, relaxing with the new experience of menstruation, understanding the possible good offered by the female body structure. Trusting in one's body includes comprehending physiologically what happens to the body of a woman each month. Knowing also includes understanding the fertility of the female body and how to use contraceptives to enable the use of that power to be expressed creatively and not destructively. Today's woman can celebrate the mystery, not from ignorance and obscurantism, but from the knowledge of exactly what happens and how potential fertility may be best used in the ongoing quest for self-identity. "You may now get pregnant" should not be handed down as a warning and a threat or as a statement to wrestle with in the bedroom in solitary fear or fantasy. It is a blessing for a future experience, a celebration of the fact that the race continues and that as women we may be part of that process in a particularly good way. Our identity as individuals may, if we choose, include the experience of pregnancy and birth.

To emerge enhanced from the crisis of menstruation is to receive an increased sense of value as an individual and the goodness of one's body structure. It heightens rather than diminishes personhood. It gives pride and status rather than shame and mistrust. For a young woman to emerge gracefully from this crisis implies her ability to understand her body in relation to her personal maturation, its value to herself and to the community, and the use of its potential so that it can be creative for herself and the community. Her trust of her body depends on her seeing it in context of the whole. In that sense it is part of the very goodness of life and of the creative structures of all living organisms. Her identity as an individual, trusting in her own body and able to experience its grace, means being able to integrate its negative and positive aspects into her personality.

Experiencing menstruation creatively is of immense importance, for it lays the foundation for resolving the next life-crises which have to do with personal selfhood and expressing sexuality to others. A woman will be unable to experience menstruation gracefully unless the family and community provide a context within which the graceful and demonic elements of the life-crisis may be expressed and her new identity as a woman celebrated. Perhaps in a time of a secular culture it is the role of the immediate family and friends to provide that context in a ritual and symbolic form since it is from them that a woman learns her sense of what is ultimately valuable in the first place.

2.

Leaving Home: The Crisis of Identity

I remember the day I left home to go to university so well. My parents came to the station to see me off. It was a bright sunny day in September and I was setting off by train at the age of eighteen to start a new life. My parents stood on the platform while I leant out of the carriage window wishing the train would hurry up and leave. As we stood waiting for those last few moments to pass making small talk to hide our mutual discomfort, I looking down at them and both of them looking up at me, shielding their eyes from the sun, I became aware of the significance of the moment. This was the beginning of a journey like none of the others, this was the beginning of my journey. It was the end of my childhood, from now on I would be on my own. My mother knew it. As the train began to move, so slowly, oh, so slowly, tears welled up in her eyes and her goodbye carried none of the usual bravado. Her emotion shook me and my excitement at leaving was tempered by sadness as I watched them recede gradually into the distance. I was on my own. There have been no other partings like that one.

This second life-crisis corresponds to what our culture describes as "adolescent rebellion" and what Erik Erikson has called the fifth stage of development—"identity versus identity-confusion." He describes the crisis as one in which "each youth must forge for himself some central perspective and direction, some working unity, out of the effective remnants of his child-hood and the hopes of his anticipated adulthood; he must detect some meaningful resemblance between what he has come to see in himself and what his sharpened awareness tells him others judge and expect him to be."[1]

From a young woman's viewpoint this life-crisis is experi-enced in terms of interpreting her identity in herself and in terms of her potential roles in society. This search for a per-sonal framework includes having a perspective on her sexuality and how it may be integrated into a whole self-image and a sense of what is ultimately valuable. This life-crisis, like the first one, is spiritual, for it involves finding an understanding of ulti-mate purpose and the goal of life on which to base a sense of one's own personal identity. The meaning of her female sexual-ity is not clear. She may emerge from the crisis of adolescence with an interpretive framework which is constructive for her future growth, or she may emerge with a false sense of her own potential and a framework which is destructive in terms of her own growth and the benefit of society.

This life-crisis involves separation and rebellion from the parental home and from prescribed social roles. It is "leaving home" psychologically and eventually physically and implies breaking with the norms and values of society and its accepted goals. For a woman, rejecting the mother, her image, and her interpretation of the female role is the deepest and often most bitter form of rebellion. She feels guilty about her hatred toward her mother, and the social framework of our culture can inten-sify this guilt. Rebellion, however, has been seen by early cul-tures as a necessary aspect of the male's journey in search of his identity. From a psychological point of view, the spiritual journey of the male away from the parental home is interpreted as a search for his masculine identity and a rejection of the maternal world in which he grew up.[2] In early mythology and religious rituals it was the "initiation" that symbolized breaking the power of the person's old world-view and the rebirth of the individual into a new identity. It involved a reintegration of elements that of old world into a whole new personal order.

For a woman, as well as for a man, it is now necessary to

break the power of the prescribed patterns of behavior and role-identification. Parents' values, their definitions of what is important about life, and their interpretations of what it means to be male and female will have to be rejected to allow for their reappropriation at another level within a personal framework. A young woman *must* reject her mother's definition of female identity in order to allow herself the possibility of formulating a sense of personal identity. Until she rejects it, she will be unable to accept those aspects of her mother and her mother's interpretation of sexuality that *are* part of herself and to integrate them into a new personal value system.

Leaving home is therefore a psychological and spiritual precondition for answering the question, Who am I? Most spiritual leaders, including Jesus, have stressed this need for separation from the natural ties in order for a new spiritual and personal reality to emerge.

"If anyone comes to me and does not hate his father and mother, wife and children, brothers and sisters, even his own life, he cannot be a disciple of mine" (Luke 14:26, NEB).

"I have come to bring division. For from now on, five members of a family will be divided, three against two and two against three; father against son and son against father; mother against daughter and daughter against mother, mother against son's wife and son's wife against her mother-in-law" (Luke 12:52–53, NEB).

A new faith, a new value structure, and a new sense of personal identity depend on rejecting and separating oneself from the home and risking the journey of self-discovery. The image of the hero setting out on a lonely voyage in order to pass through trials and sufferings in quest of his individuality is a common theme in literature and mythology.[3] Far less frequent is any corresponding image of the young woman setting off on a journey to find her identity in and through the various events of her voyage. In earlier times a woman's identity was perceived to be given with her sexual identity and her biological role. Initiation rites for a young man symbolized his new identity as a male, the death to the old self and the resurrection of the new.[4]

Mircea Eliade suggested that there is no new state without the annihilation of the old, and in archaic thought a male's identity appears to be *made* rather than given.[5] A male must therefore "die" in order to be reborn, "made new."

The lack of similar initiation rites for women appears to reflect an idea that a woman's identity is a given in her nature and is gradually revealed to her through the stages of her sexual development.[6] Her identity need not be "made" since it is inherent. Mircea Eliade described the difference between male and female initiation rites in primitive societies in that

for boys, initiation represents an introduction to a world that is not immediate—a world of spirit and culture. For girls, on the contrary, initiation involves a series of revelations concerning the secret meaning of a phenomenon that is apparently natural—the visible sign of their sexual maturity.[7]

For most primitive societies no further initiation is required for a girl after puberty although sometimes stages of female initiation correspond to the developmental stages of her sexual powers: menstruation, defloration, marriage, and the first childbirth. Each stage is a further development of the female sacred creative power gradually being revealed. "In Gisu society, as in most such societies, a woman's role is to bear children, so that the development of her physiological power to do this is marked at various stages, to control and augment it."[8]

Even in cultures where ritual ceremonies accompany later stages of sexual maturity, Eliade suggested, there is no idea that a girl needs to be "initiated" any further after puberty.[9] She does not need to be "reborn"; she is revealed as being a "creatress," and her procreativity places her in contact with an inherent feminine sacredness that is revealed to her during initiation.[10]

In these primitive cultures a woman's identity can be found in and through her role as a mature sexual being and is directly linked with the sacred creativity of life that she experiences in her body. In our contemporary society a woman's identity is not found in the sacredness of her role as childbearer. No longer is her role in procreation perceived as the numinous power of the universe operative through the female. The role of men and of women in conception is known to be equal, and her childbearing role is not perceived as being linked with the sacred power of her fertility. Her identity as a woman is no longer given, that is, defined by her sexuality and the potential of her body as it relates to the sacred power of fertility.

In primitive societies a woman's identity as childbearer is not merely a personal role but is "transpersonal." The understanding of the sacredness of fertility gives the woman a view of her role in her community and her purpose in life that is linked to transcendent power. Her value for the community is ultimate. In our modern societies fertility no longer has that sacred value, and a woman cannot find that transpersonal framework and identity with the ultimate purpose of life in and through her biological role as childbearer. A woman too must be "reborn" in the sense of finding her personal meaning. With no understanding of a *necessary* sacred cosmos, a woman, just as a man, must experience a psychological death and rebirth and must construct a framework of ultimate meaning in shaping her identity. She too must shape her destiny and accept the fact that there is no natural passage from the maternal world to her future role within it.

The young woman today experiences on a level similar to that of young men the ambiguity of this necessity to shape one's identity, and yet she also experiences an inability to choose. Many of the deepest anxieties of young women during this life-crisis involve the lack of models. The ability to find total identity in the roles of wife and mother has been seriously undermined by the delayed marriage and limited childbearing common in our culture and the increased longevity of the woman. Who am I? must be answered knowing that there are few guidelines. Most fundamentally a woman must come to terms with her sexuality as a creative aspect of her identity at a time when the predominant culture assigns little value to the femaleness of her body.

A woman in our time experiences some particular fears about

this life-crisis. Leaving home is perhaps harder for the young woman than for the man. At some level the girl knows she will need to find an identity which includes making a choice about that option elected by her mother, namely childbirth. She is often tempted to believe that she need not negotiate her own world-view and her understanding of herself. Fearing indiscriminate use of the power of female sexuality, her family and society will often try to block her growth into autonomy and freedom and keep her dependent and protected either by ushering her into an early marriage or by keeping her emotionally bound to parental ties.

I stepped out of the drug store holding my small package with an immense feeling of accomplishment. That small rubber implement, my diaphragm represented a major step for me. I felt very good and proud of my ability to take responsibility for my own sexuality. How kind life had been to me! After that 'near miss' I had realized how imperative it was for me to get my own method of birth control. I was very nervous as I waited for my appointment with the doctor I had selected from the yellow pages. I had felt as if everyone in the waiting room was looking at me, knew that I was there under "false pretenses". Having been taught all my life that pre-marital sex was wrong, at least for a "good" girl like me, finding myself there in that New York doctor's office to be fitted for my diaphragm was quite a challenge. I felt guilty. I lied and told the doctor I was about to be married. Luckily he didn't ask too many questions. I suspected he knew anyhow. Surely he could tell from my nervousness! As I stood on that baking New York street, my diaphragm in my hand, all the anxiety of the trial faded away. I had known what I had to do and I had done it. It was a major step in my life: to know that from now on I could take responsibility for my own sexuality without the fear of unwanted pregnancy. I felt I had conquered the world!

The young woman experiences ambiguity concerning leaving home, for leaving implies loneliness, risk, and taking responsibility for oneself and one's body. Separation from the secure world-view makes one vulnerable and confused about how to make choices, what to do, what paths to follow, which relationships to pursue. The fear of freedom is connected in the life of every adolescent with making mistakes and the lack of approval from society. To know who I am, I must take my search seriously, and, though I am afraid, I must explore all elements of my life. Women in this society have not been taught that they too have a spiritual quest, that they shape and mold their self-identity. It is harder for a woman in our culture to trust her freedom, to actualize her powers and risk herself. On one level her fear comes from her sexual vulnerability. She *must* wrestle with the responsibility for her procreative potential. She must deal with her identity and how it relates to the expression of her sexuality. Who am I? for a woman is not identical with her sexual role, but it cannot exclude a consideration of it and a decision about its potential expression.

The reality of female sexuality leads many young girls to respond to the ambiguity of the adolescent life-crisis by assuming a false identity. Identifying oneself with one's body is no longer a graceful option in our world but represents a demonic solution. Erikson calls it a "false ideology," a meaning system to which one turns to avoid the risks and confusion of the crisis stage. It is not a true resolution but represents being overwhelmed by the terrors of making choices, the fears of responsibility.

A young woman often turns to her sexuality to protect her from the implications of this identity crisis. She defines herself in terms of her attractiveness to boys and focuses all value in her need to be loved. Her sexual attractiveness thus becomes the totality of her identity, and she is unable to trust any other element of her personhood, either her physical, intellectual, or creative powers. She has no sense of self-worth but is defined from without by the response that men give her. Her sexuality is manipulative since it is expressed, not from self-love, but out of a desperate need to find identity in being loved. Her sexuality often seems to rule her, for she lacks any self-understanding and purpose except in the immediate moment. This type of solution is socially condoned and reinforced by advertising and the media. It is destructive because it fails to recognize that personal identity cannot be given by others.

While a woman's sense of herself may be enriched and strengthened in and through relations with many others, no one aspect of herself can bear the weight of her total identity. No one person can supply her total framework. Teenage marriages have such a poor success rate because they often represent, not the mature resolution of the identity crisis, but an attempt to find a haven from it.

Another false solution to the crisis of identity is never to leave home. This option is also accepted and encouraged by mothers and fathers as appropriate behavior. Staying close to parental influences and internalizing and fulfilling the hopes and desires of parents in dress, career choices, selection of male friends, recreation activities, sexual behavior; in a word, to be a "good girl" represents a response of fear to the life-crisis of adolescence. To stay "mama's girl" or more frequently "dad's girl" represents an unwillingness to break away, to take responsibility for oneself, to endure the pain and anxiety of acting without guidelines or parental approval. It is a demonic solution because it represents a regression, a pretense that there will be no necessity to formulate one's own value system and shape one's own life. It symbolizes a lack of trust in the self and a lack of trust expressed by the family and the community in the autonomy of the individual. Following the wishes and internalized standards of the parental home may indeed function for a while as the young woman follows the approved social roles. In the future, however, the questions of personal identity and sense of ultimate purpose in life must reemerge and be renegotiated, sometimes at great cost for herself and her personal relationships.

Finding one's identity in the intellectual aspect of oneself and focusing on one's mind to the exclusion of one's body can also represent inability to deal with self-definition. This resolution often emerges from the pattern established by the first crisis, menstruation. In her early experience of her body the girl internalized an attitude of shame and distress to her sexuality. Lack of trust in her body and its sexuality led her to resolve the adolescent crisis by placing all her emphasis on the development of the mind and her intellectual powers. She becomes career oriented in a manner that expresses an exclusive goal in life. Her intellectual strengths and dedication are built on high hopes for the future but also compensate for a lack of satisfaction in her sexuality. She is fundamentally vulnerable in her desire for and inability to negotiate mature sexual relationships. Distrustful of men and of her own body, she is yet lured by the power of instinctive sexuality and finds herself torn by passions that threaten to undermine her intellect and her self-image.

This option may function successfully for a time since it provides a goal in life that can sustain a young woman for several years. The development of the intellect as an exclusive goal will not answer the question of identity for a man or for a woman. Negotiating the meaning of one's sexuality may be sublimated for a while, but it will reemerge at a later stage, sometimes in a manner most destructive of the pattern of self-identity already established.

A version of this form of resolution in earlier times was the choice to enter the religious life. To enter a community of women, to see oneself as an individual primarily defined by one's spiritual being and rational self, to retreat from the world by taking a distinctive form of dress or life-style, consciously choosing the path of celibacy, without coming to terms with one's sexuality, resolves the adolescent crisis with a false ideology and false sense of identity. To dedicate one's life totally to the service of God and to others in the name of God or to give up one's life for others with a view of the ultimate value of that self-sacrifice can be as personally uncreative as trying to find one's life in service of a husband or in search of sexual satisfaction. It is based on a belief that the meaning of one's identity as a woman can be defined by others, can be submerged into the identity of another, even God. It fails to accept the reality of one's sexuality, to negotiate it in relation to its expression to others, and to refuse to accept the limits of one's physical structures.

To identify oneself with pure spirit and to see one's role as the servant of that spiritual power certainly provides a transcendent framework and goal, but it finally avoids the issue of personal responsibility for shaping one's destiny and the necessity to accept the ambiguity of one's freedom. If you conceive your life to be ruled by God or Krishna, your role is to follow his commandments, but it doesn't necessarily imply having wrestled with the implications of one's sexuality or having come to terms with the responsibility of negotiating a sense of ultimate value for oneself.

All these options represent a lack of sufficient self-trust to negotiate the major tensions of adolescence. Because of the particular historical role of women and because relationships are a necessary aspect of a woman's sexual self-expression, women's fears during this crisis often center around the thought that they will never be married or that they will never find anyone to love. To recognize that negotiating personal relationships is an essential part of the life-crisis of the young woman does not imply either that young men are not also deeply concerned about their sexual relationships or that a woman's identity is to be *defined* by her sexual relationships. The particular nature of female sexuality and its relational implications will be discussed in the following chapter. At this point it is sufficient to point out that male psychologists have often been led astray by the certainly important relational drive in women and have defined total female identity by it. Thus Erikson can write

. . . young women often ask, whether they can "have an identity" before they know whom they will marry and for whom they will make a home. Granted that something in a young woman's identity must keep itself open for the peculiarities of the man to be joined and of the children to be brought up, I think that much of a young woman's identity is already defined in her kind of attractiveness and in the selectivity of her search for the man (or men) by whom she wishes to be sought.[11]

Likewise Bruno Bettelheim writes: "As much as women want to be good scientists and engineers, they want, first and foremost, to be womanly companions of men and to be mothers."[12]

What women really want, I hope, is to be whole, and in this wholeness a true identity and a sense of ultimate worth may be found. A woman's vulnerability in her sexuality often causes her to ignore her other creative aspects, her intellectual, artistic, and physical powers. Women are particularly prone to solve the crisis of adolescence by submerging themselves into another. Relationships with others *are* essential elements of a woman's self-discovery, but no one of them offers the solution to the question of her identity or an ultimate value by which she can define her life.

I have never been very good about loneliness. When I was first in New York I didn't know many people. The men I knew in graduate school seemed not to want to date me and the girls in the dorm weren't interested in doing things I wanted to do. One day I got tired of waiting for someone to do things with and decided to go alone. So I set off into New York, myself and I, went to the Metropolitan Art Museum, had lunch at the very pleasant restaurant and bought myself a ring at the museum shop. In the evening I went to the Carnegie hall and heard a concert by Rostropovitch. As the day wore on I began to experience a deep sense of pride in myself. I could have a good time alone. I watched the people, relished each special sight and sound, aware of my growing sense of enjoying my own company. In the evening tired after a long day I returned to the dorm. The girls asked me where I had been. "Who did you go with?" "I went alone." They could not understand it, how could anyone enjoy themselves all alone? It was a wonderful day. It put me back in touch with myself. I still have that ring, my present to myself. Whenever I feel lonely and depressed and unable to enjoy life, I look at that ring and remember my promise to myself to find joy in my aloneness.

The ability to experience the crisis of adolescence in its positive as well as negative implications and find a framework which can provide a basis for satisfaction of one's life purpose lies in taking on and recognizing the quest for autonomy. In risking herself the young woman can experience new strengths in the use of her freedom, stretching the boundaries of her powers to the limit and immersing herself in new activities, new relationships, and new journeys. It is a time for travel, physically and spiritually, and for testing new forms of understanding, new roles, and new behavior. This breaking new ground may be painful for parents and society to watch, for there *is* real danger involved. Just as in primitive initiation rites the young men's journey away into the bush or the girls' seclusion from the community involved the very real possibility of death or being physically or mentally maimed,[13] so in our society the young woman's journey to test her reality involves many dangers. She may get lost and confused and lose herself in destructive causes or relationships or under the influence of others. She may suffer great loneliness and fears and opt for a quick solution to her pain.

Nevertheless, the young woman who embarks on her journey away from home with a healthy degree of confidence in her worth and a trust in her powers cannot be destroyed by the hardships and ambiguity. As she engages life in the many aspects it presents, she will discover a greater sense of worth and a greater ability to know what she wants. Taking responsibility for herself, financially as well as ethically, will give her a clearer sense of what is ultimately valuable for her and enhance her sense of trust in her own perceptions of reality. Intellectual challenge, financial survival, responsibility for sexual behavior, finding new friends and relationships, new tests of physical strengths, are all aspects of this creative experimentation in order to discover one's particular personal meaning structure. There will be failures, choices that lead nowhere, experiences which appear destructive and unproductive.

We cannot protect the individual from these failures; indeed it is necessary that she undergo them, for without some loss nothing new can be born. This does not imply that growth happens only through suffering or that the journey is essentially tragic. The view of woman's journey as inherently sorrowful is a common theme among male writers of the late nineteenth and early twentieth century. Caroline Heilbrun in her book *Towards*

Androgyny described the image of "woman as Hero" found in the literature of Ibsen, James, Shaw, Lawrence, and Forster as one who suffers and symbolizes a tragic image. The woman was hero for these writers in the sense that

... the hero begins with a purpose he believes himself sufficiently in control of circumstances to carry out; but to be human is to act on partial knowledge; and so events he could not forsee, the past which he has forgotten, rise up to thwart him. He undergoes a passion, he is acted upon, he suffers. He emerges from this suffering with a new perception of what the forces are which govern his world. We all know, or soon learn, what it is to think that we can plan for the future, what it is to learn at last what past acts—our own or other people's—were at work to render impossible our illusion of being in control of destiny. This action—purpose through passion to perception—which the hero undergoes is a universal, perhaps an archetypal action.[14]

The woman's journey through the life-crises is no less and no more inherently tragic than the man's. The crisis imposes new opportunities, new strengths, and new freedoms, and it closes some options and sees the failure of some hopes. Coming to terms with our physical and intellectual limits and recognizing that we are not able to be totally undetermined is in fact the true meaning of freedom. Personal freedom means maximizing one's potentials within the limit of a particular personality, unique skills, and body structure. The woman embarking on the quest for self-identity is not an essentially tragic figure, caught up by life and determined by events that shape her destiny. Crisis is natural to life, as is change. Discovering identity and acquiring self-trust implies a belief in one's creative freedom that gradually recognizes the real rather than the illusory possibilities and limits for its expression. The rewards and regrets of personal discovery are found in making choices, in limiting oneself to one area of study rather than another or one relationship rather than another, in fact, in actualizing choices. For the young woman as well as the young man, loss of security and a sense of being determined by events or the failure of plans is one aspect of the creative redefinition of value-structure.

The spiritual dimensions of this life-crisis involve entering the creative and destructive aspects of the process of self-discovery. Finding a framework within which to answer the question, Who am I? is a spiritual quest, for it involves making a judgment about the meaning of life as a whole and how one's life relates to it. Erik Erikson is correct in seeing that these value structures are not necessarily "religious belief systems" but that they function for the individual woman in the same manner. Her ability to reach an understanding of who she is, what her purpose in life is, and what roles she will play in society depends upon an internal sense of the valuableness of her life in relation to the whole. She may not be conscious that she has this value structure, but it in fact defines what is "holy" to her as well as her personal and ethical choices. The value frameworks of some young women may be very limited, making them unable to integrate the diverse aspects of themselves for future development. These are demonic options because they affect not only the individual girl but also her relation to others. They ignore the whole self and fail to recognize the implications of personal freedom and identity.

A graceful experience of the crisis of youth would be to emerge reborn with a new creative interpretation of one's world and aim for life. It would mean coming to a sense of one's value structure that utilizes one's unique strengths. Trusting in the self and finding pleasure and purpose in one's new capacities involve accepting and finding satisfaction in being responsible for one's choices. This implies being aware of one's limits and yet having high hopes for the future. To emerge from the crisis of youth with an increased sense of trust in one's body and mind and its relation to a sense of ultimate value is to find grace in that experience. "Leaving home" becomes therefore a critical stage for the pattern of future life-crises. A young woman can be strengthened by it and enhance her sense of self and trust in the world or she can be constricted and limited by it.

Though the outcome of the second crisis may often appear negative, the human spirit has great resilience. I agree with Erikson's perception that though a life-crisis may not be creatively handled at the time there is a future potential for the vital ego capacities of the individual to reemerge and rework aspects of earlier unresolved crises.[15] If a young woman emerges from adolescence with a lack of trust in her intellectual powers and her feelings of sexuality, all is not lost. Some elements of the personal whole may be reintegrated at a later stage. Erikson's studies of an exceptional individual such as Luther are an example of how later resolution of the unresolved adolescent crisis proved finally productive. Contemporary women who later in life discover their hidden artistic talents, their intellectual powers, or an ability to trust their sexuality are resolving aspects of an earlier crisis. Hope is never lost. However, the need to reintegrate an aspect of the whole self that has been ignored in earlier stages can only take place at greater cost and danger to the self and others. Radical shifts in midcareers, the breakup of marriages, and experimentation with sexual relationships are attempts to reintegrate earlier stages of self-development. The increased cost of this reintegration is due to the major commitments both in personal and financial terms that have already been made.

For some the ability to reintegrate never really occurs, and that potential of the self is always lost. To spiritually leave home and to begin the process of discovering one's true identity is thus a vital step in developing a rich and meaningful life. Perhaps we need new forms to celebrate our new freedom, to usher us on our way, words and actions that can symbolically represent the dangers and the promises of our new identity. The graduation dance is a poor substitute for a family or community action to send young women and men on their way and to symbolize affirmation and trust in their need for the journey and the possibilities it promises.

3.

Sexual Maturity

When I was a teenager I used to look at adult men and women and think they all "do it." I used to look at my parents' bed and think they do it. My thoughts at that time about intercourse were not all that pleasant, I used to watch dogs mating with curiosity and no little sense of disquiet. There is no knowledge which separates the girl from the woman more radically than knowing the secret: what it is like to have intercourse. That first time is charged with anticipation, all those years of wondering and now finally this is it! The mixture of feelings is intense, being an anticipation of great pleasure and a fear of possible pain, all culminating in the question, what will it feel like? I suppose no actual experience of sexual initiation could live up to the hope of absolute bliss imposed upon it. Ignorant of my own body, I did not know what my potential was. My lover, not much more experienced than I, practiced coitus reservatus. I was very puzzled. My overall feeling after it was over was, Is that it? Is that all? I was deeply disappointed at not being shot toward the stars in orgasmic ecstacy—whatever that was. My sexual inauguration was inauspicious, at best.

Why is sex a life-crisis for a woman? To some extent all sexual experience is a crisis in that it involves ultimately risking the self in the deepest and most intimate form of contact. The first experience of sexual intercourse and initial sexual contacts are critical and far-reaching in their implications for future sexual experiences. The life-crisis of sex for a woman is more than just the generalized attitude toward her identity or her sense of trust in her body, it is a particular crisis associated with becoming sexually mature. This experience is sometimes called "losing one's virginity" or "defloration." It is an event that a young girl long anticipates with hopes and with fears. The focus of her attention is not orgasm but the entry of the penis into the vagina, an experience for which she has no counterpart. It is a moment which marks, perhaps more irrevocably than menstruation, her feelings of having become a woman.

The ability to experience the first intercourse as pleasurable and not as painful depends, not only on the state of the hymen, but also on the whole context of the event. The girl's hopes and fears, her bodily inexperience, and unawareness of her sexual feelings, as well as the usual lack of sensitivity and experience of her partner, all conspire to make the first intercourse in this culture an emotionally and sometimes physically painful event in the life of a woman.

The first intercourse is well recognized by cultures more primitive than our own as an event of particular spiritual danger and significance for the girl. The many rituals of "defloration" express this perception that the first act of intercourse is sacred, to be handled with care, and involves many dangers. In some societies it involves cutting the hymen or ritual defloration by a group of men.[1] In every case defloration is dangerous for the male as well as for the female and must be carried out with ritual precautions.[2] Ritual defloration is often seen as a sacrifice to the god of the hymen which is sometimes performed by the priest of the temple or a stranger, who represents the god.[3]

The medieval custom of the *droit du seigneur* in which the lord of the manor took responsibility for deflowering the local brides was a continuation of this attitude that the first act of intercourse was a "dangerous" and sacred event.[4] The act of defloration is not only dangerous from the point of view of the male involved, but more fundamentally it marks a major change in the life of a woman. While the male may need to protect himself from the potentially destructive aspects of being the one who brings the female into sexual maturity, it is a life-crisis for the woman involved. Erich Neumann commented that the first sexual encounter "is for the feminine destiny, transformation, and the profoundest mystery of life,"[5] and "for the feminine, the act of defloration represents a truly mysterious bond between end and beginning, between ceasing to be and entering upon real life."[6]

Entry is indeed the most important moment of intercourse from the woman's viewpoint. Psychologically it is the most important because it is the act of opening oneself to another at the point of greatest vulnerability. The extreme risks involved led many cultures to dedicate the act to the god or his surrogate, who performed the function. It was a sacred event when Roman brides "deflowered" themselves on the erect phallus of the statue of the god Priapus in order to offer their hymens to the god and to pray for the fruitful outcome of their fertility.[7]

This ritual dedication of the first intercourse has implications for us although in most cases young women today do not experience bleeding or necessary physical pain during the first act of intercourse. Simone de Beauvoir wrote that it is the *fact* of penetration that is of far greater significance than the experience of pain.[8]

Woman is penetrated and fecundated by way of the vagina, which becomes an erotic center only through the intervention of the male, and this always constitutes a kind of violation . . . it remains an act of violence that changes a girl into a woman; we still speak of "taking" a girl's virginity, her flower, or "breaking" her maidenhead. This defloration is not the gradually accomplished outcome of a continuous evolution, it is an abrupt rupture with the past, the beginning of a new cycle.[9]

The crisis of the experience of sex for a woman occurs, not only once in the first act of intercourse, but has to do with the whole issue of her attitude toward her body and toward her sexual experience. The particular nature of female physiology and the responsibilities of childbearing imply that a woman has certain fears that arise from having these sexual structures. Whereas a man may fear castration, the woman's fears focus on violation. Since her sexual apparatus is internal to her body, she "is entered," and her fears have to do with the nature, timing, and context of that entry. Taking the penis into oneself has a psychological impact involving the totality of the body. It becomes part of the deepest center of the woman and in that context involves the whole person.

That is why particular fears are associated with the first intercourse. Trusting is the major issue. For a woman to have a satisfying sexual experience, for her body to be physically ready for intercourse, she must reach a stage of physiological, psychological, and emotional readiness. Being ready means relaxing and trusting the man and the whole context within which the sexual act occurs. Writers often speak of woman being a psychosomatic unity and that her totality is involved in each act of sexual union.[10] This is partially due to the female physiology, the location of the vagina within the body. Although we now know that the clitoris, located on the outside, is responsible for a large degree of sexual arousal, actual penetration is a necessary source of pleasure and satisfaction, both for the male and for the female.

The totality of the woman is involved in intercourse because the potential outcome, childbearing, involves the totality of her body and self. In spite of the pill and sterilization, a woman's sexual experience is still implicitly connected with the natural biological potential of intercourse, namely pregnancy. Though precautions may have been taken, in every case a woman has to wrestle with the responsibility for her body's potential. Though a corresponding male pill may be developed, the very fact that the woman bears the children means that this concern for contraceptive responsibility can never be felt on the same level by a man as it is by a woman. Since her body is involved, she always has to *know*. She has to take precautions; she must think about it since she will bear the potential outcome of that act in her body.

This unequal physiological responsibility between men and women accounts, I believe, for the particular nature of the woman's fears concerning intercourse and her experience of the meaning of trust. The responsibility of a woman for her body involves its procreative potential. That fertility involves the whole self, changes the whole self physically and psychologically, and brings new life into the world. Each act of intercourse, even in this day of the "fool-proof" pill or in later years after menopause, may take place in total trust only when the procreative issue has been physically and thus emotionally resolved. That is why trusting and relaxing involve a decision about the total context of the act of intercourse, not only the trustworthiness of the man, but the readiness of one's body for that implicit total commitment. The woman's anxieties and her fears about a sexual encounter revolve around the totality of commitment which involves her soul and (potentially) her whole body in more than one event.

Vulnerability is therefore one of the deepest fears a woman may have about her sexuality. This is why the crime of rape has such enormous psychological impact. To force entry, to take possession of a woman's body at that point, is a form of attack unlike any other. A woman cannot remain emotionally uninvolved in the experience of rape because it is a forcible attack into herself, into her deepest body structure that involves the totality of her self-identity. Rape is as much a psychological as a physical crime since it involves not only bruising the woman's body for a man's sexual satisfaction but violates her selfhood as a woman and as an individual.

The rise in the incidence of rape in modern society speaks, not of sexual liberation as a culture, but of increasing fear and hostility toward female sexuality on the part of men. The issue of trust in sex for a woman is implicit in the realization with which she lives, from childhood to old age, that she may be raped. She must protect herself; she is taught not to trust strange men, dark streets, or even those she knows. A woman must not put herself into compromising situations; she must not be alone at night, journey alone, or drive alone. She must always take precautions. The issue of the safety of her body and her sexual structures is always in the back of her mind. A woman may learn karate and assume an air of confidence, but deep down she knows she is compensating for what is not given in her body structure.

Overcoming fear, being able to trust, finding a person, a place, and an emotional framework within which to express the totality of her sexuality is the greatest issue in the life-crisis of sex. Perhaps this is why women do not appear very successful at depersonalized sex. While pure eroticism without personal commitment may be an element of female experience, women appear more concerned with the emotional depth and intensity of the sexual encounter although the feelings may not endure over time. It is very difficult for women to separate emotional feelings from sexual satisfaction. To be totally involved in the passion of the moment is to be able to place all other thoughts and cares aside, at least for the time being.

Women may seem able to "fake it," but they know the deep pain and emotional cost of "making love" to a man when love and trust are not involved. They feel divided, split in two by discordant feelings and actions. Body actions signify oneness and mutuality; the head and heart scream the opposite. The emotional long-range implications of this form of sexual experience intensify distrust and feelings of fragmentation. A woman who concludes intercourse in tears (often to the bewilderment of the man) is acting out the pain of her inner confusion.

To be divided is the worst form of pain a woman can experience concerning her sexuality. To "make love" to a man she does not love, to pretend erotic attraction and arousal, to carry a child she does not want, to have sex with a man against her will are forms of spiritual female death. They involve a fundamental self-deception and destroy the true feelings and any ability to experience real satisfaction from the event.

One of my most painful experiences of being divided was when our month-old baby began to cry during the initial stages of love-making. The crisis in me was radical—a call from my newly separated biological offspring, perhaps needing food from my breast, while my erotic attraction was focused toward my husband. It would have been better to stop and attend to the baby and then return, but I did not. It's difficult to describe how that cry seared through me in the middle of a loving embrace. I was divided between two claims on my sexuality, and the baby's cry was the more insistent. The pain I felt in trying to block out that cry and being unable to do so was intensified by proceeding through the sexual act. I was being untrue to my real feelings; I was violating myself by my lack of self-trust.

The experience of sex for a woman is therefore not only a matter of trusting the man but of trusting herself. Her sense of timing, her body feelings, her erotic readiness, and her desire for the entry are essential for her ultimate satisfaction and for the satisfaction of the male. Because signs of male sexual arousal are so obvious, she tends to rely on his body and respond to his advances rather than knowing and trusting her own. The lack of knowledge the woman has about her body and about what gives her pleasure and the lack of responsibility for her erotic satisfaction are ancient legacies of an attitude toward the female body which regards it as fundamentally asexual, an instrument through which the man enjoys himself and babies are born. A woman has a responsibility to her body, not only to take care of its procreative potential, but to own its inherent possibilities for giving and receiving pleasure. To be proud and aware of her bodily possibilities implies awareness of her sexual feelings and an ability to communicate that awareness to others. In this regard it seems to take many years in our culture for a woman to experience the fullness of her sexual potential. Is this because of some physiological limit or because it takes so long for a woman to learn about her body, trust its feelings and her desires, and most importantly to share them with her partner in complete self-expression and sexual enjoyment?

The signs of sexual arousal are less visibly obvious in a woman, the clitoris more hidden than the penis, and the pattern of sexual arousal may appear slower initially (usually due to psychological rather than physical factors)[11] though more sustained in the long run. These differences in the pattern of sexual response or arousal necessitate a woman's being aware of her physical feelings and being able to explore their potential with her partner. What is fundamentally at stake is trust of her bodily processes and her ability to express them. To be one, physically and emotionally with herself and with the man, is the goal of all sexual satisfaction and personal wholeness.

I suppose that week I feared I was pregnant was the most frightful week in my life. I had a photo taken for a passport during that week and I look as if I had aged ten years. I can never look at that picture without remembering the emotions of that week. When my period was three days late I began to panic. I told my lover that I feared I was pregnant. I remember the day, it was a glorious spring day in New York City and we walked along under the trees in the park by the river. The beauty of the day made the reality of my situation seem even worse. We will get married, he said. We can have a nice wedding. I can get my friends and relatives over. I was so grateful that he showed concern and a sense of responsibility but it was all too ridiculous. There was no way we could get married, being, as we were, both students in a foreign land. I didn't want to marry anyone under such circumstances. I knew what I had to do. I knew with every bone in my body that there was no way that baby could be born. It would have meant the end of my tenuous existence in a foreign country, the end of my graduate studies. There was no money, no family to fall back on. There was in my mind only one choice open to me, illegal though it was. Abortion. As the days passed and my pregnancy seemed inevitable my determination increased. I was not concerned with the morality or immorality of the act. I knew that for me in that situation there was only one possible action. My worries were focused on how to find information and how much it would cost. When my period returned three days later, I was amazed since I had already accepted what I thought to be inevitable. I have never regretted having lived through that week. I know what it feels like to be unalterably opposed to the reality of being pregnant.

The experience of being divided in oneself, either out of a desire to please or out of fear and mistrust, becomes most critical in the matter of an unwanted pregnancy. To experience the fetus as quite other than oneself is a natural element of pregnancy. To be hostile to that fetus, to be unprepared physically and emotionally, to be *irrevocably* divided is, however, destructive for the life of the woman, for the pregnancy, and for the life of the potential child. The wish to abort comes from this experience of unalterable self-dividedness. Irene de Castillejo in her book *Knowing Woman* writes persuasively of how it is possible for women to seem so hard-headed at the initial stages of pregnancy

For a great many women a foetus of only a week or two holds no emotional appeal. Death in any case is part of life. Woman, who is so intimately and profoundly concerned with life, takes death in her stride. For her to rid herself of an unwanted foetus is almost as much in accord with nature as for a cat to refuse its milk to a weakling kitten.[12]

Until a relationship is established with the fetus, an abortion, spontaneous or therapeutic, while it may bring guilt and regret, is perceived as a better option than allowing the fetus to develop to term. To choose an abortion is a sign of fundamental untrustworthiness of the whole personal and social context for that pregnancy. To delay abortion is dangerous, however, not only physically but personally.

A woman . . . who is determining *not* to carry an unwanted child is split in two, her mind refusing to follow the dictates of her body. Every day's delay accentuates this split. The obstacles put in her way permeate her with a guilt which is not basically hers, but is projected upon her by society. On the other hand every day the foetus which she could have aborted lightly with no harm to herself and without offending her nature, is nearer becoming a child who claims her love. . . . I am convinced that from this artificially induced split many a woman never recovers.[13]

Male theorists who fear that women will resort to abortion instead of birth control do not understand the difference between *within* and *without*. To remove a growing organism, a potential child, from a woman's uterus, even in the early months of pregnancy, involves a qualitatively different form of risk and decision than using birth control. The fact that many women in our society experience an unplanned pregnancy as a traumatic event creating the deepest ambiguity about the fetus speaks, not of their moral failure as individuals, but of the social framework of our culture. We value free sexual expression for men and women, but condemn the single woman as guilty and her offspring as a bastard.

A woman who feels the necessary anxiety to consider abortion correctly experiences the distrust of our society as a whole either toward children born out of wedlock or in her personal moral integrity. She does not trust the context for bringing the fetus to term, either in terms of the financial, social, or personal situation. To ask a woman to bear a child knowing that she will have to give it up for adoption is to ask her to perform a high act of courage and to transcend the stigma placed on her. She must be glad and not ashamed and welcome the developing child in order to give it away. In this society that possibility for self-trust and valuation is hard to achieve since, although babies are now needed for adoption, we do not value those who bear them outside marriage or give them up within marriage. To experience a pregnancy with shame, haunted by anxiety and fear for the future of the child and oneself, is to be essentially divided against oneself. In that context an abortion, with all its emotional risks, appears the better option and the more responsible solution.

The spiritual crisis of sex for a woman is fundamentally concerned with trust, of overcoming fears, and of taking responsibility for her sexuality. To experience her body as divided from herself, determined by the other, is to experience it demonically. The crisis for a woman in all sexual experience is that trust involves being open to the other, allowing oneself to be vulnerable. If that trust is given, then the experience of sex becomes graceful; something more is given and received through that physical and emotional union than has been put into it on either side. The body can become for the woman in all aspects of sexual experience, but particularly in sexual intercourse, the best teacher of what we have called grace. Something new is created when the woman abandons herself to the totality of mutual sexual interaction between herself and her lover. She is full of her sexual desire and strives to express it completely in and through her partner. She is not passive to his sexual desire but a full giving-and-receiving participant.

The grace of this encounter is experienced partially through the individual physical satisfaction of each partner in orgasm but more fundamentally perhaps in the renewal of the two through the totality of the mutual encounter. The emotional and spiritual impact of the event transcends its actual experience; it brings peace, a feeling of oneness in the self and with the other, and a new self-trust and mutuality. The possibility of experiencing sex as a graceful encounter beckons us ever toward it. Overcoming fears and trusting in her feelings, in her body, in her lover, and in the whole context of the event are for a woman the preconditions for being totally present and thus able to experience the wholeness or healing aspect of sex.

Finding the graceful element of sex implies not wanting anything from it. If sex serves some other emotional need than itself, it fails finally to provide it. Women as well as men often use sex to make themselves feel loved or wanted. The physical closeness of sex does not create the bond of mutuality. In this culture we promise too much, for sex is seen as the panacea for all ills, particularly for loneliness and feelings of personal inadequacy. Rollo May in his book *Love and Will* described accurately our attempt to use sex to *make* ourselves feel:

Another motive is the individual's hope to overcome his own solitariness. Allied with this is the desperate endeavor to escape feelings of emptiness and the threat of apathy: partners pant and quiver hoping to find an answering quiver in someone else's body just to prove that their own is not dead; they seek a responding, a longing in the other to prove that their own feelings are alive.[14]

When an individual woman looks for identity through sex, she manipulates its power and will be unable to experience its graceful and transforming aspects. If sex is perceived as a power that the woman uses to control and entice a man, it is being used to overcome self-distrust. Sex can also be commercialized or employed as a weapon against men, but this use increases a woman's sense of alienation and destroys her sense of wholeness. Sex is therefore not a personal power but an aspect of biological givenness, our rootedness in a process that goes beyond us and which may, if we trust it, bring us to deep harmony with others and create new forms of personal wholeness.

The fundamental crisis in the experience of sexuality for a woman occurs because sexuality in its essence transcends itself. It points beyond itself literally in its biological outcome and figuratively in terms of its ability to create new life, new depths of communication with another, and new levels of self-understanding. A woman's ability to experience sexuality as graceful depends, I believe, in not identifying herself with any particular sexual role or function and in not denying the implications of her sexual body for a continuing sense of self-identity. This balance is particularly hard for women in our culture to appreciate. A woman is not a sex object, a baby machine, a wife, or a mother. To the extent that she identifies herself with any one or some of these roles she demands that one aspect of her self carry the weight of her whole identity.

Perhaps the most familiar demonic interpretation of sexuality for a woman lies in a tendency to submerge herself into one element of her sexuality. The graceful experience of sexuality involves a perception that a woman's identity cannot be located exclusively in being loved, in being able to bear children, or in being a wife or a mother. The failure of our culture is that we have no image of female identity that includes and yet does not exclusively identify a woman with any potential expressions of her sexuality.

Earlier cultures had an understanding of the relationship between the identity of a woman and her body that corresponds to what I call the graceful experience of sexuality. The image of the "virgin" in Egyptian, Babylonian, or Greek cultures was not a sexually uninitiated woman but a female who was "one-in-herself," not defined by her role as daughter, wife, or mother, though indeed she might be involved in all these roles. The Virgin Goddess worshiped by these cultures is associated with the moon and is described by Esther Harding thus:

> The chief characteristic of the goddess in her crescent phase is that she is virgin. Her instinct is not used to capture or possess the man whom she attracts. She does not reserve herself for the chosen man who must repay her by his devotion, nor is her instinct used to gain for herself the security of husband, home and family. She remains virgin, even while being goddess of love. She is essentially one-in-herself. She is not merely the feminine counterpart of a male God with similar characteristics and functions, modified to suit her feminine form. On the contrary she has a role to play that is her own, her characteristics do not duplicate those of any of the gods, she is the Ancient and Eternal, the Mother of God.[15]

This sense of autonomy is particularly appropriate for woman in the contemporary search for selfhood. Her spiritual identity is her own, and though she may be lover, wife, and mother, not one of those roles or aspects of her sexual expression defines her identity.

Worshipers of the Moon Goddess or the Great Mother ritually dedicated their sexuality to the sacred power of fertility in a ceremony called the *hieros gamos* or the "sacred marriage." These rituals included an act of sexual intercourse with a priest or a stranger in the temple when the woman sacrificed her virginity and dedicated her power of fertility to the Great Virgin Goddess.

The context of these rites is strange to us since we have no concept of the sacred power of fertility or a sense of needing to dedicate our sexuality in its procreative power to any cosmic purpose. There is an element of this ritual, however, that remains symbolically important for us in that it is a recognition by the woman that her sexuality, even in its nonprocreative expression, is not a personal power to be exploited and used to satisfy ego-needs. Through this rite the woman recognizes her "virginity" and her spiritual autonomy and acknowledged the meaning of her sexuality within that context.

A woman can be driven by a lack of sense of self to use her sexuality as ego-fulfillment and thus manipulate her sexuality to fill personal needs and insecurities. Harding suggested that the rituals of sacred marriage represented a transformation of a woman's attitude toward her sexuality and her instincts. The ritual signified that a woman's sexuality was not her own but a manifestation of the creative life-force itself.[16] This recognition enables a woman to view herself as whole. Her sexuality is an essential aspect of the creative power of life embodied in all of us, but uniquely in women; it is hers and yet not hers. To the extent that she perceives this relationship of sexuality to identity, she will experience her sexuality as graceful and not demonic. If she looks to sexuality to solve her questions of identity, she will not only fail to experience her body as enriching her knowledge of herself and her relations with others, but she will find identifying herself with her sexual nature ultimately unsatisfying.

The body is a great teacher and is one of the most immediate forms of experience available to all humans. Sydney Janet Kaplan comments that Doris Lessing's heroine Martha Quest achieves profound personal discoveries through the experiences of sexual relationships, pregnancy, and childbirth. "Sexuality itself becomes inescapably linked with the search for knowledge in these novels."[17] As Lessing portrays her heroine, sexuality must indeed be linked with continual growth to a higher consciousness, to a deeper form of self-understanding.[18] Insofar as a woman allows herself to experience her sexuality to the fullest, to trust the bodily processes, she will experience them as bringers of "knowledge" that may serve to strengthen her sense of unique identity.

The crisis of the early years of sexual maturity in the life of a woman involves gaining a perspective on the experience and expression of her female body and its relation to an ongoing sense of identity and purpose in life. To reject one's body as irrelevant or only negative in its implications for selfhood is to fail to find grace within one's physicality. Equally destructive would be to attempt to find oneself totally in one's sexuality.

Sexual intercourse and the other experiences of female sexuality can be graceful if fear can be overcome with trust. Our female sexuality can then reveal a quality of existence found in our bodies that speaks of the creative, renewing, and loving aspect of all life.

4.

Love

As I walked along the street I felt really attractive and happy with the world. I was wearing new clothes and it was a bright day with a delightful crispness to the air. I saw him some distance away walking towards me in a cheerful way. He was so good-looking and was wearing a bright red waistcoat that I had never seen on him before. I knew we would stop and talk, and as we came closer together there was that half-smile on both our lips that acknowledged the inevitability of our meeting. What warm flirtatious words we exchanged on that pavement! Where are you going, he asked me. "To buy a pair of rubber gloves." "May I join you?" And so we walked along; I was certainly aware of a growing excitement inside. When he said, let's go for coffee, I was glad. Over coffee we talked for what seemed hours about ourselves. He asked me about myself and my story. He listened so well and with such understanding. I felt very close to him. At one point he looked at me and said "Is there something going on here, something happening between us"? Yes, I think so, I said. I had been watching him from a distance for several weeks and now it was clear. We walked slowly home, both I believe, somewhat awed by the new knowledge, the beginning of love that had been revealed between us. Outside the apartment I gave him my phone number on a piece of the brown paper bag containing the rubber gloves that I had carried all that way. We

lingered long in each other's presence unable to tear ourselves
away. When I finally got upstairs to my apartment, my heart
was racing. I felt so wonderful, I felt I was in the process of
falling in love with him.

Love is a crisis! Erik Erikson in *Identity: Youth and Crisis*
describes the first crisis of adulthood in terms of finding a capacity to form intimate relationships:

Sexual intimacies often precede the capacity to develop a true and
mutual psychosocial intimacy with another person, be it in friendship, in erotic encounters, or in joint inspiration. The youth who
is not sure of his identity shies away from interpersonal intimacy or
throws himself into acts of intimacy which are "promiscuous" without true fusion or real self-abandon. . . . he may settle for highly
stereotyped interpersonal relations and come to retain a deep "sense
of *isolation*." If the times favor an impersonal kind of interpersonal
pattern, a man can go far, very far, in life and yet harbor a severe
character problem doubly painful because he will never really feel
himself, although everyone says he is "somebody."[1]

Erikson suggests that the capacity for forming a mutual relationship of trust with another is not defined by sexual experience. Love is not sex, nor is sex the same as love, though
their implied relationship is one of life's greatest challenges. In
speaking of love here, I do not necessarily mean marriage but
the experience of an intimate, trusting, and open relationship
between two adults in which there can be a sharing of true
identities and a mutual devotion and care which can overcome
antagonism, fear, and distrust.[2] The crisis character of loving
involves overcoming one's fears and moving into a trusting relationship with another; the possibility for loving is threatened by
many false concepts of the meaning of relationships. We can,
as Erikson suggests, identify intimacy with sexual encounter, or
we can identify it with popular understandings of love such as
"falling in love." To judge from the persistence of popular
myths concerning women, the romantic image of love may be a
more powerful influence on the minds and hearts of women
than on men in our culture. The typical romantic image of the

woman "in love," in its purest form, is the magazine picture of the young bride dressed in white. She is the symbol of ideal love, a woman transformed by happiness.

The concept of love that we frequently have in mind in this society, however, can lead to destructive, stereotypical relationships, far removed from those that enhance the individuality of two persons. "Falling" in love may feel wonderful and provide a total focus for one's existence. "Love" happens suddenly; like a force that seizes us from the outside, it sweeps us up and surprises us by its intensity and vividness. This experience of "being in love" is essentially passive; we don't know when it will happen or why. We find ourselves in love, totally absorbed by this other, ecstatic when we are with him or her, and anxious and lonely when we are separated.

Denis de Rougemout in *Love in the Western World* suggested that this kind of love is *essentially* tragic; it thrives on separation and pain and idealization of the other.[3] While I think de Rougemont has somewhat overstated his case, I agree with his conclusion that romantic love as we understand it is a poor basis for marriage. And yet this is what we all desire: "Love and marriage go together like a horse and carriage!" Indeed, love and marriage do go together, but the interpretation of love and the roles that men and women assume within the image of "being in love" lead, not to happiness ever after, but to a sober challenge to grow beyond romantic love. We need quite a new understanding of the meaning of an intimate relationship and one's identity within that relationship. Many of us fail in the attempt, as the divorce rates indicate.

"Falling in love" is what Erich Fromm calls a form of pseudolove: a symbiotic dependent need that is appropriate for a relationship between parent and child but inappropritae between two mature adults.[4] The romantic image of falling in love leads to what many psychologists have described as destructive forms of dependency and projection between the partners. To idealize, to yearn for, to long for the other, to believe that one could not live without the other is what we assume "being in love" is all about. The reason our popular concept of love is so potentially demonic for the woman in this culture is that it encourages her to surrender her very being to another. I believe that women are particularly prone to believe this myth and to live in expectation of the day when they will fall in love. When love goes and the image of absolute bliss dissolves, we feel cheated that love did not make us happy ever after.

The powerful mythology concerning love that our society has adopted operates, in my opinion, in a particularly distinctive manner for women. The experience of "being in love" has essential dangers for a woman that will often lead her to interpret love demonically and to express her love to others in a destructive, manipulative fashion. The demonic element of love is, in my view, distinctively experienced by women, not because of anything essential to their biology or psychology, but because of the lack of a positive self-image. Patricia O'Brien comments that "most women still don't realize they have a potential for separate psychic existence, which involves taking primary responsibility for one's own emotions and adjustments to life."[5]

The dependency that women have on the need to "fall in love" is connected not only with their lack of self-confidence but with their identification with the traditional passive role of the woman in sexual initiative. Percival Symonds suggested that

women seek love experiences for the restoration of wounded self-esteem. Love serves as a compensation for the inferior sex role they are forced to play. Since a woman does not play the aggressive sex role, she has to prove that she can attract men.[6]

Another version of the power of the romantic image of love is that women define themselves *in terms of their relationships* with others. Judith Bardwick suggests that girls are distinctive from boys in that what a boy achieves through separation and autonomy a girl achieves "through intimate connections with others because her identity is defined *through her attachment to others.*"[7] This view of the relational identity of women is connected with the image of woman in our culture as the "goddess of love." She not only inspires men to love, but she herself *needs* loving in a manner distinct from that of men. A woman is more in need of love and protection, more vulnerable to love, and, in her very essence, more essentially able to give love than a man. This traditional image finds expression in many levels of literature, both religious and psychological. In their interpretation of female psychology, Jungian psychotherapists, for example, perceive women as needing love to reveal their true nature, both to the other and to themselves.

Erich Neumann in his analysis of the Greek myth of *Amor and Psyche* suggests, for example, that this story represents the truth that "feminine individuation and the spiritual development of the feminine . . . are always effected through love."[8] The view that a woman gains awareness of her true identity through love is connected with the idea that female identity is largely instinctive and unconscious and that a woman needs to relate to the masculine phallic power to open her up to her true sexual identity and ability to love.

Every healthy woman has a deep need to submit to a benevolent phallic power, to receive and contain it. The instinctive feminine reaction (attraction, fascination, fear and withdrawal) to the sword-like aggressive phallic power, has the effect of transforming the penis into an instrument which opens up a channel for the circulation of Eros. Without the help of her instincts, a woman is unable to mediate the union in love which she needs, and which the man also needs.[9]

While this perception acknowledges that men also need women, it presupposes that a woman's spiritual and sexual development rests on the erotic power of love.[10] However, for an individual woman to look to love for identity and to see herself as nothing without the "transforming" power of phallic force represented by a particular male is, I believe, a distortion of the meaning of love and woman's search for identity in relation to love. We all need love in one way, for none of us discovers our individuality except in tension and interaction with others. For a woman to believe that her physiology makes her in some way more relational, more in need of others, and more able to give in relationships is, I believe, to abstract from physiological function a fundamental psychological distinction between men and women.

Women are indeed at the present more prone to see themselves as defined by their relationships, particularly by their "love" relationships, because of the lack of valuation that our culture has placed on the uniqueness of female identity. Female identity and male identity are both realized in and through interaction with others. Men do "need" women to discover themselves in and through radical physiological and emotional encounter with others who have distinctive perceptions of reality because of their unique individuality, which includes their female body space. Women do "need" men, not merely to fertilize their bodies, but also to encounter others who have significantly distinctive physiological, emotional, and psychological experience. It is in my mind a fallacy to define women, because of their need for men to impregnate them, as more *essentially* determined in their identity by their relationships to others, whether in the form of love, marriage, or childbirth.

In his analysis of "Womanhood and Inner Space,"[11] Erik Erikson is wise in assuming that wholeness of the self depends upon integrating the particularly unique aspects of female physiology and potential into an ongoing growth toward identity. In my opinion, however, he overstates his case, in assuming that a woman is defined by her "inner space" and that the essential aim in her life journey is to find a male who will fill that inner space: "Womanhood arrives when attractiveness and experience have succeeded in selecting what is to be admitted to the welcome of the inner space 'for keeps.' "[12]

According to this theory, a woman is thus "empty" until she finds a man whom she can trust; she is more vulnerable in love, more dependent on the male than he on her, psychologically as well as physiologically, and has a sense of lack of worth while her inner productive space is void. Erikson suggested that it is the female experience of a potentially creative inner space that leads also to a woman's greatest vulnerability:

Emptiness is the female form of perdition. . . . To be left, for her, means to be left empty, to be drained of the blood of the body, the warmth of the heart, the sap of life. How a woman thus can be hurt in depth is a wonder to many a man, and it can arouse both his empathetic horror and his refusal to understand. Such hurt can be re-experienced in each menstruation; it is a crying to heaven in the mourning over a child; and it becomes a permanent scar in the menopause.[13]

This form of interpreting the relation between female physiological experience and the personality of women distorts the meaning of female identity and relationships. It suggests that a woman is more open, more vulnerable, and in greater need than man to be loved, to be filled by another, in order to realize her true nature. Women have indeed traditionally defined and been defined by others, by their relationships, their loves, their marriages, and then their children. In my mind this form of understanding the relationship between love and identity for a woman is particularly limiting and leads ultimately, *not* to a sense of personal security and identity, but to a further crisis of personal meaning at a later stage in life. Judith Bardwick comments that

it is dangerous for a woman's sense of worth to be enormously dependent upon her husband's reactions to her. . . . In a very real way girls achieve identity when they marry and when they have children—but when their most important functions in that role dissolve, they have an identity crisis.[14]

The dependency that women exhibit first on love and later on marriage and children to give them a sense of ultimate self-worth, while endorsed by cultured stereotype and psychological perspective, offers, in my opinion, a false view of the relation between women and love. It enhances the view that a woman is passive, dependent on the other for self-trust. From the psychological point of view it encourages a view of a woman's role in love that is masochistic and dependent and that lacks responsibility for selfhood. It is a constricting condition, not only for the *woman*, but also for the one who loves her. If her essential being is defined by love and her vulnerability is so great, then the male is doomed to fail. He can never love her enough; he can never fill her up; no man, no child can fill that crying empty space. The image of woman as a devouring monster, swallowing the male into its own depths, that we find in traditional mythological images such as the Medusa and the Gorgon may come from man's experience of woman as insatiably dependent upon him for her very being.

The distance between us was unbearable. I felt as if I had never been so lonely in all my life. It was a time of much self-pity and I cried many tears into my pillow. My love was thousands of miles away and I lived daily waiting for a letter or phone call. Those were terrible phone calls. I would lie in bed after midnight and talk to him sometimes for an hour or more. The worst was when I tried to tell him how I was feeling. I would cry on the phone and tell him how much I missed him. There were long silences also. All I could hear was the breathing at the end of the phone. When I told him I loved him and longed for the time we would be together I felt as if my blood was spilled out onto the ground. I was vulnerable, helpless, dependent on his love. Talking to him on the phone was sometimes worse than not calling. It increased my sense of complete isolation. After we hung up I would cry and cry at all the feelings left unsaid, the enormity of the distance between us and the terror of my own loneliness. Loving him was the source of my deepest pain and my greatest joy. I lived for the days when we might be together. All my energy was directed to that moment.

The deepest form of personal crisis for a woman may be to find a balance between independence, both physical and psychic, and interdependence. Her physiology suggests identifying herself with her female body functions: needing the other to protect, to fill, to give her a sense of self through her relationships. A woman's particular demons may thus be more linked with trying to find herself *in* love, in marriage, or in childbearing. To be totally other-directed, to "define oneself by one's relationships" is fundamentally to miss the uniquely personal identity that a woman has been given. It misses the essential responsibility of the whole self to the self in finding its own way in life and

in developing its creative center in all areas of life. Risking in
relationships is an essential aspect of creative self-discovery; so
is being alone, testing one's self in relation to all areas of experience. Women in this culture are so vulnerable to traditional
images of female success, and they are so accustomed to evalu-
ating themselves in terms of falling in love and getting married
that they tend to undervalue their achievements in other areas
of experience and will in fact avoid success if it threatens the
attitude of men toward them.[15]

A fundamental problem that women face in determining the
relation between love and identity and finding a graceful dimension to love is the attitude toward self-love that has been proposed by generations of Christian culture. Self-love has been
identified with the deepest sin, the antithesis to true love.
Women have been particularly prone to the destructive effects
of this view of self-love as inherently evil because of the image
of woman as more capable of self-sacrificial love. Luther, for
example, thought that self-love must be sinful. "So thou doest ill
in loving thyself. From this evil thou art delivered only when
thou lovest thy neighbor in like manner—that is, when thou
ceasest to love thyself."[16] Irving Singer comments that Luther's
interpretation of the second commandment is far surpassed by
the Jewish interpretation that assumes self-love is not only natural but good.

A sound morality must take account of our own interests equally
with those of others. Hillel expresses himself in the spirit of the
principle when he says: "If I am not for myself, who is for me? And
when I am for myself only, what am I? And if not now, when?"[17]

We often conceive of self-love as "narcissistic" and selfish
and fail to see that selfishness constitutes not an overabundance
of love for the self but a lack of trust in one's self. Edward
Edinger comments that

narcissism in its original mythological implications is thus not a
needless excess of self-love but rather just the opposite, a frustrated
state of yearning for a self-possession which does not yet exist. The
solution of the problem of Narcissus is the fulfillment of self-love

rather than its renunciation. . . . Fulfilled self-love is a prerequisite to the genuine love of any object.[18]

This lack of self-love causes men and particularly women to distort the meaning of love and to look to "falling in love" to make them happy. The traditional definition of woman as essentially more loving, more relational, causes women in this Judeo-Christian culture to see loving another as something one "does" for the other rather than the genuine expression of a mature personality that cares for itself, respects its own needs, and affirms the essential value of its unique humanness. As Erich Fromm so clearly points out in his discussion of self-love in *The Art of Loving*, the lack of self-love, the expression of a full creative character, causes the distortion of love. Love of the self *is* the basis of love of others.[19] Until woman can rid herself of an image of loving that is based on a notion of "unselfishness" and self-sacrifice and the essential "givingness" of her role, she will interpret love demonically for herself and those she loves. The tragedy of this image of loving is that it has been sanctified and blessed by generations of Christian tradition as well as by psychological perspectives on women. This ideal of woman as essentially loving is summed up in its typical Christian form by a statement of Pope Paul VI in 1966:

For us, woman is a reflection of a beauty greater than herself, the sign of a goodness that appears to us as having no bounds, the mirror of the ideal human being as conceived by God in his own image and likeness. For us, woman is a vision of virginal purity, which restores the most lofty affective and moral feelings of the human heart. For us, she is, in man's loneliness, the arrival of his companion *who knows the supreme gift of love, the value of co-operation and help, the strength of fidelity and diligence, the common heroism of sacrifice.*[20]

If a woman internalizes this concept of herself, she will play a passive role, even a masochistic one, and will fail to take responsibility for her selfhood as an individual with essential value. Until she loves herself, her loving will be manipulative, dependent, and destructive of the freedom of others since it will not spring from an active, alive, and potent attitude toward the self and the world.[21] Without this attitude, we tend to "fall in love" and remain passive in face of its romantic vision. Women are led to believe in this ideal, and their dependency on the myth reflects a belief that they are nothing until somebody loves them. Romantic love begins, not from a sense of wholeness and self-trust, rather

one person projects some part of himself which he values highly onto someone else, where he adores it. He then begins to act as if this person were an extension of himself. Longing to enjoy the misplaced part of himself, he clings to the person on whom he has projected it, he is possessive and jealous, he delights in the loved one's presence, but feels anxious and incomplete when this person is absent. . . . this is nevertheless the kind of feeling the American has in mind when he says "I love you."[22]

Putney and Putney's analysis above explains why women appear more vulnerable to the myth of romantic love and more dependent and passive within love relationships. The desire to "fall in love" is not the cry of the empty inner biological spaces but the cry of the empty female soul that knows not itself, trusts not itself, and finds no strength in its own potency. Faced with their lack of a sense of a creative center, women look to relationships to give them identity. Giving themselves in love represents too frequently, not the giving of a full creative individual, but an attempt to achieve selfhood *through being appreciated as one who gives.* Erich Fromm expressed the view that the ability to give stems, however, not from living for another, but from having something to give.

What does one person give to another? He gives of himself, of the most precious he has, he gives of his life. . . . he gives him of that which is alive in him; he gives him of his joy, of his interest, of his understanding, of his knowledge, of his humor, of his sadness—of all expressions and manifestations of that which is alive in him. In thus giving of his life, he enriches the other person, he enhances the other's sense of aliveness by enhancing his own sense of aliveness. . . . the ability to love . . . presupposes the attainment of a predominantly productive orientation; in this orientation the person has overcome dependency, narcissistic omnipotence, the wish to exploit others, or to hoard, and has acquired faith in his own human powers, courage to rely on his powers in the attainment of his goals.[23]

This statement strikes me as more profoundly spiritual than the traditional Christian images of the loving and giving woman. The concept of self-love as the basis for the ability to truly love others *is* present with the Christian traditional although it has not been applied to women and their role in relation to God, man, or children. Meister Eckhart expresses this view that self-love will lead to true love of others

if you love yourself, you love everybody else as you do yourself. As long as you love another person less than you love yourself, you will not really succeed in loving yourself, but if you love all alike, including yourself, you will love them as one person and that person is both God and man. Thus he is a great and righteous person who, loving himself, loves all others equally.[24]

Loving oneself is not easy. Loving oneself implies an act of faith and trust in one's potential wholeness. Loving oneself means not looking to others for this absolute sense of self-worth and believing in the creative potential of one's personhood. Loving oneself also implies forgiving oneself, accepting the fears, the insecurities, the weakness. Loving oneself means recognizing one's needs and being able to accept conflict, separation, change. "Love is a willingness both to place demands upon and receive demands from another person."[25] Loving oneself is an act of faith because it means letting go of all notions that we are acceptable or worthy by reason of our "being for another"— mother, father, lover, child, or ultimately even God. Loving ourselves as women implies not only the ultimate risk of accepting ourselves and trusting our particular creative center but breaking through the stereotyped images of the female role in relationships as all-loving and self-sacrificial. It means breaking through the internalized self-definition of the nature of woman as inherently more giving to an acceptance of one's personal growth goals as a sacred trust. Loving oneself is an ultimate risk for women, for it means finding a sense of personal worth as an individual which is not reflected in the cultural images of woman or what gives the female social status in Western society.

If this is the basis for truly mutual love, how many of us will ever attain it? Psychologists such as Abraham Maslow describe this state as being "self-actualized."[26] Mature love is therefore a mutual interaction of two people who turn to each other, not out of a sense of need, loneliness, and self-hatred, but out of a sense of full personhood. This form of mature love is based on a one-to-one encounter and of necessity transcends the stereotypical roles assumed in male/female relationships. It reflects interaction between two equal persons who recognize the freedom and dignity of the self and the other.

Perhaps it is wiser to suggest that true love exists not as a fixed state dependent upon our achievement of psychological maturity. Personal wholeness is not a condition we achieve through our efforts or through the efforts of others. The ability to trust oneself and to accept the dark and incoherent aspects of the personality is itself an "act of faith." Faith in the self as well as in another is ultimately a risk, an act of courage. This form of ultimate trust and self-acceptance, while not contrary to reason, can never be produced by reason, and in that sense is a gift. This is what I mean by the experience of grace in love. To be a true self and to be able to risk that self in a mutual relationship with another depends on being fully present in the encounter. We are not divided in ourselves; we know our strengths and our weaknesses, and we have accepted them for what they are. Possessing this sense of the ultimate worth of our identity, we can then see the other for what he or she is, be certain of the ultimate goodness and worth of that individual personality, and trust in the unchangeable quality of the core of that identity.[27] This is the experience of love as a gift, as transforming, not in the romantic, idealistic sense, but as a meeting of two individual selves.

Irene de Castillejo writes perceptively of this quality of the "self" in meeting. "Mutual service without betraying one's own deepest truth is the paradox at the very centre of the art of living."[28] She suggests that wholeness and love go together and that giving, tenderness, and understanding, the qualities that we have often associated with loving, do not always heal or make whole. Love is ultimately not something that we can learn to do although we can create the conditions in which love can light upon us.[29] This process of learning is growing into awareness of who we are, uncovering and expressing the totality of ourselves so that we can be whole in a relationship.

I am not equating love with the Self, though I am convinced that wherever there is love the Self, our symbol of totality, is the link which holds the two who meet together. The meeting in every case is the presence of the Self . . . love is more than the meeting. At the meeting is the presence of the Holy Spirit.[30]

The possibilities inherent within this form of creative meeting include affirming and renewing the strengths of the woman's individuality, sensing deeply her self-acceptance, and integrating all elements of her personality into a developing sense of herself and the relationship. "This potentiality for personhood, which is always latent in woman, is completely fostered and reawakened in a woman who exists in a B-love relationship [B-love is love for the being of another, not based on need fulfillment] with a man who is capable of that type of love."[31] In real loving she can transcend the roles and become a person.

The experience of meeting *does* have a transforming power, and it does give us an enhanced perception, a more honest and true sense of ourselves. The graceful dimensions of the experience of love are the same for men as for women. For a woman, however, the fears and risks in loving and the potentially demonic interpretation of her role in love are particularly connected with the fears of coming to terms with her selfhood. Risking love in this culture may mean that a woman must deal with her anger, jealousy, and hatred. It is perhaps more difficult for women to be aware of these feelings and not to feel guilty for having them since women have been told to see themselves as all-loving. Knowing herself and knowing and articulating her more destructive feelings toward the one she loves may be a woman's hardest task. Finding the ability to express the whole of themselves in relationship is indeed an act of courage for many women, long-schooled to repress the negative feelings and demands and to live up to the role-image. Distinguishing between the needs of the other and one's own fears is particularly hard for women.

Love is indeed not a state that we are "in" or "out" of. It comes as a gift when we risk ourselves, our *whole* selves, in relation to the other. In that meeting artificial roles and traditional male/female behavior expectations disappear, and we feel free to be as we are. The crisis character of love is, as Erikson suggested, that we as women will get trapped into an image and understanding of the meaning of our identity and its relation to love that may continue for many years and fail to give us an experience of our selves as whole individuals in relation to another. By accepting a concept of pseudo-love, we will be cheated of the experience of humility and thankfulness that comes in the meeting of two in what Martin Buber called an "I–thou" encounter.

The misinterpretation of love and its relation to the meaning of the personal identity of the woman is demonic in its effects on a woman's attitude toward herself in the succeeding stages of life and discovering her identity within them. It is also self-deceptive in that a woman loses touch with her autonomous "soul" and places responsibility for what she feels in those who form her relationships. It is unproductive finally in the sense that it cheats her of the real power of a loving meeting to bring a new sense of self-disclosure and self-affirmation, a renewal of the self in reciprocity and warmth and mutual sharing with another. This is the graceful experience of love.

5.

Failure and Loss

Before madness, the person is crude, self-made and self-sufficient. After it, she is taken up by two élite societies—the dead inviting her to die, the unborn requesting to be born. Between these rival importunities she draws, for a time, her breath.[1]

This passage is taken from *The Bell Jar,* Sylvia Plath's autobiographical novel of a young girl's descent into insanity. Commenting on the imagery, Mary Ellman points out that Plath saw the body as a cage and felt that the mind was a bell jar. Sylvia Plath's personal story ended in suicide. The value of her writings for contemporary women is that she describes with such force the failure of hope, the experience of disillusionment, and the frustration common to many women. Sylvia Plath tragically found no way out of the breakdown of hope except to end her life. The experience of the death of hope and the death of the self is part of all our lives. The spiritual question that arises is whether we will be consumed by that death either by committing physical or spiritual suicide or whether there is a way through the darkest nights to rebirth.

One may experience the failure of hope at many different levels and at various points during life. The collapse of a long-term love relationship, radical defeat in terms of vocational choice or goals, and the death of parents and friends are the failures and losses common to early adulthood. A miscarriage,

65

the death of a child or spouse, the breakdown of one's marriage, illness, lack of career advancement, financial disaster, retirement, and children leaving home are failures of hope common to later stages of life. For each of us, men and women, this type of crisis is not something that we pass through once but many times, leading to the final crisis, anticipating our death. The first experience of this kind, however, is a particular trial because of the intensity of its force. It *can* destroy us and send us irrevocably into a despair from which we never emerge. Reckoning with death in life, death in the sense of this radical experience of the end, becomes one of the most significant tests to human identity and the growth into maturity.

While it may seem that the more time that has elapsed in human investment and commitment, the harder will be the experience of loss for the individual, it is rather the failure of hope earlier in life that proves more devastating. The death of a friend or a parent, the failure of love, or the discovery of an incurable disease may be more traumatic because the failure of hope is greater; there are fewer memories, and the identity of the individual is more critically tested by the experience. William Goode suggests, for example, that divorce is often more traumatic in short marriages than in long ones because long-term relationships tend to become more casual and their breakdown is less "soul-wrenching."[2] Similarly, widowhood may be far more difficult for the younger woman than for the older because far greater and dramatic changes in life-style are necessitated for the younger woman.[3]

Each of us, at whatever stage in life must encounter the experience of failure and loss. For the younger woman the crisis is likely to be intense, and the questions raised by it for the continuing formation of her life, her sense of herself, and her life choices tend to be critical. The rise in suicide rates among younger people symbolizes not only of the failure of our society to provide adequate support but also the desperate feelings and the failure of hope among youth and their tendency to be consumed by despair.

I was very unhappy the first week of my marriage. I noticed that a week after we were back from our honeymoon that my husband no longer kissed me as he left for work and returned. He was very matter of fact and busy and all the affection and tenderness that we had known during our engagement was gone. I was very bitter. Does it take a week, I said to myself, does it take only a week! Walking the streets of that dusty little town, knowing nobody, with nothing to do except to cook meals and play wife, I poured my energy into making nice meals, baking cakes and trying to create a sense of coziness in that little apartment. It did not work. I hated the place, I was deeply depressed. When his sister arrived two weeks later to sleep on the couch in the living room, her presence intruded on our sex life since the walls were paper thin. My resentment at her intrusion into our tenuous state of married existence, changed to relief as I began to see her as a distraction from my growing despair. Our premarital love and passion had evaporated and my expectations of married bliss had vanished into the air. In its place reigned resentment, loneliness and anger. Unable to express those feelings to my new husband or to myself I sank deeper into a state of cold despondency and a sense of having been cheated by life.

Sorrow and suffering of this intensity raise the question of my own identity most fundamentally. The element common to all forms of loss and failure is not only the end of my hope, my relationship, or my way of life, but it is the end of *myself*. I die; the structure of my world is no longer the same; I have failed; I feel there is no point to living at all. Robert Neale calls these experiences "death in life."[4] They are the times when my sense of trust in myself, my self-worth, and the nature of my world are most dramatically challenged.

Women experience these times in our particular society most frequently with respect to their relationships. The end of a marriage and the death of a spouse are more traumatic for many women than men because of the greater amount of personal identity that women have invested in those relationships. Similarly discovering that she is unable to have children, having a miscarriage, or losing a child through death are forms of personal tragedy for a woman that involve the totality of her body and her self-image. It is not that women by nature suffer more than men, but in terms of our social order women have more limited forms of personal valuation and thus place more of their identity into relationships.

For men the more traumatic experiences are the loss of a job, bankruptcy, or retirement. The crisis raised for a woman by the failure of love, the destruction of a marriage, or the death of a spouse is intensified by the fact that being alone is particularly difficult for women in this society. Living alone or thinking of oneself as unmarried is a most trying experience for the mature woman. Women are not taught to trust their own aloneness or to trust other women as supportive companions.

Women are reared now as they have always been in this country, with the spoken and unspoken assumption from the cradle that they will marry. . . . In contrast, a man is raised with a sense of what he is to be, not whom he is to marry, and he is therefore identified by what he does. . . . A woman is identified by whom she marries.[5]

Since woman's identity is particularly bound up with her relationship to a man, the failure of love, divorce, or widowhood may be the most critical times of personal death that a woman encounters. The depth of the crisis is tied up with the fact that women distrust their sense of female sexuality. The end of a relationship undermines and disrupts, not just a way of life, but the sense of oneself as a woman. "Almost without exception [women] report having felt *something less than a woman,* and the first [new] date is expected somehow to make them feel more like a whole woman once again."[6] This distrust of herself as a woman also reflects social attitudes toward female sexual identity which perceive the single woman as threatening to society.

The more successful or independent a woman becomes, the more afraid society is that she has lost her femininity and therefore must be a failure as a wife and mother. She is viewed as a hostile and destructive force within the society.[7]

People disapprove of women without men, not in an overt way, but by exhibiting a vague, general cautiousness toward what is not known or understood.[8]

The end of a relationship can represent for the woman a most radical feeling of failure in terms of herself as a woman and her role in society. As with any death, women feel not only a sense of failure but a sense of guilt. While there is guilt concerning the children left fatherless, particularly in cases of divorce, legal structures enhance the guilt-producing aspects of divorce.

Society practically forces divorced people to define their experiences in terms of blame, failure, and guilt. Almost all of us were brought up believing in marriage as the ultimate goal, the final problem-solver, the preordained institution in which we would live out our lives, each partner being everything to the other. Society sees to it that we pay the price for having denied the truth of this ideal picture.[9]

In this passage Mel Krantzler has described the social pressures which affect the experience of the end of a marriage in divorce. These feelings of guilt are particularly true of women since women have found more of their identity in terms of their relationships with men. Society has seen women's roles often exclusively in terms of their roles as wives and mothers.[10]

Why did my marriage fail? As I now understand it, the very basis of the marriage represented not my whole self, but my search for security. Having been raised in a "keep sex until marriage" framework I assumed that since I had a sexual relationship with someone that must mean I was fated to marry him. I think I was very insecure about my female sexuality, so glad that at last someone was taking an interest in it. In that experience I forgot all my other interests and strengths and tried to sublimate myself to his interests. I was not able to be whole in the relationship. We did not share a common outlook on life or even the meaning of marriage. And yet I had loved him. I think my disappointment at the failure of that marriage is that the love I had towards him turned to resentment and finally, in my despair, to hate. What had I done to deserve this?

There *is* death in life. The failure of love, the end of a marriage, the loss of hope are as much a death as the actual death of a spouse or a child. The sense of failure, guilt, and sorrow associated with grieving for the dead are all emotions common to and appropriate for these other forms of death in life.

The ability to emerge from the experience of death in life with a rebirth of hope and with a strengthened sense of personal identity depends on being able to experience fully the feelings associated with that loss. We are now discovering that grieving after the death of one we love is a necessary and important element in the healing process. Mourning is not evil, rather "the ritual [of mourning] itself is effective in moving the widow into an institutionally desired limbo location outside of ongoing life, without which re-engagement in new roles and relations would not be possible."[11] If the ritual of mourning is appropriate at death, then mourning is also appropriate at the end of relationships. Divorce is a death which should be followed by a period of mourning, coming to terms with emotions, loss, and so on.[12]

Our society has no ritual forms to express sorrow, loss, and personal crisis outside of the funeral. Lacking some community or social structure for this appropriate expression of emotions we drive one another deeper into feelings of personal failure, despair, and loneliness and prevent the transformation of the self into hope. In our relationships with one another we need to help people experience their despair, not by consolation or building up false hopes, but by allowing others and ourselves to plumb the death of the self in all its hopelessness. In writing of the role of the counselor in suicide prevention, Robert Neale in *The Art of Dying* suggests that the only way to prevent suicide is to permit it. The counselor needs to share in a death vigil with the one in such despair. In giving up hope with the individual, we allow the death experience to create a new life.

At this point there is time and space to consider life and death and to discover the seeds of a new community, a new self, and a new relation to God. Man has always known that true transformation never begins until one reaches the point of absolutely no hope—the "sickness unto death."[13]

All forms of personal despair lead implicitly or explicitly to the question of suicide. Even those of us who have never experienced the depth of despair in a consciously suicidal manner are aware of this loss of all hope. There is a possibility for utilizing these crises in a positive, creative, graceful manner, whether they are events of personal failure, a death, a divorce, or a disappointment in career. The only way to emerge strengthened from despair is to go into it. James Hillman, writing of the strategy of suicide prevention, comments that there must be no false hopes but an emptiness of soul and will.

It is the condition present from that hour when, for the first time, the patient feels there is no hope at all for getting better, or even for changing, whatsoever. An analysis leads up to this moment and by constellating this despair lets free the suicidal impulse. Upon this moment of truth the whole work depends, because this is the dying away from the false life and wrong hopes out of which the complaint has come. As it is the moment of truth, it is also the moment of despair, because there is no hope.[14]

A woman whose life seems destroyed by the end of a marriage and whose basic sense of herself is radically shaken cannot pass simply to a new life and a new identity. This crisis is a painful and deathly experience in which the question of personal identity and the meaning of life is raised once again. To despair is not to respond demonically, rather to turn in one's anxiety and loneliness toward substitutes and panaceas for the pain is more destructive in the long run because it is a sign of our lack of trust in a perspective that the darkest moments can lead to a new sense of ourselves. A deceptive solution to being left alone is to try to maintain the pattern of a married household by having brothers or mothers move in as substitutes for the lost relationship, a common practice among widows and divorcees.[15] Unless a woman can begin to face herself as an individual alone, not defined by having someone to look after, she will be unable to utilize the possibility offered by the crisis, and she will be unable to discover new life.

Another tempting solution to the end of relationships common among women in our society is to give way to the social pressure to prove oneself sexually. "The assumption seems to be that because I am a divorcee, I'll go out with anyone, I'm so desperate."[16] To prove to oneself that one is worthwhile, a real woman, by turning quickly to casual sexual relationships is ultimately self-defeating and marks a failure of self-respect and trust in one's sexuality. Sexual satisfaction alone cannot fill the void and provide the necessary redefinition of the self. Giving in to the pressure to remarry or quickly to find another relationship is another self-destructive solution particularly common in our society. There are strong pressures for remarriage after divorce and widowhood. Being a woman alone, raising children alone, and finding satisfactory sexual relationships outside of marriage are all difficult socially or emotionally, and the financial pressures are real.[17] The formlessness and the lack of a socially acceptable role for the single woman in this culture make life hard for the never-married and the once-married.

. . . *by the very fact that there are no such provisions* [for consequences of divorce], *no set of status privileges and stigmata, which would allow the divorcee to play easily the mother role outside marriage,* the institutional patterns create pressures toward new marriage. . . . There is thus as yet little direct institutionalization of postdivorce adjustment.[18]

There are also no socially expected roles in this society for a widow. In earlier societies and in societies where there are more extended kinship systems the older women perform functions in terms of the whole society and suffer the death of a husband in a less traumatic manner.[19] In our own society widowhood is often characterized by a total loss of identity, "relegation" to an all female society, and a descent into apathy. Widows also turn to remarriage for companionship and a relief from loneliness.[20]

The crisis of being alone is real for a woman in this society. The only possibility for a graceful experience of such a significant loss is through recognizing the potential that the crisis offers for a new perspective on one's individuality. To accept one's individuality for what it is involves an attitude toward the self that is particularly hard for women to discover.[21] However, the gradual emergence of a sense of self-respect and a belief in oneself as a unique person, not the quest for happiness, will allow the individual woman to experience renewal through the destruction of the old identity. Discovering one's uniqueness involves letting go of the internalized cultural stereotypes of what it means to be a woman. Mel Krantzler comments:

Those divorced persons which felt that the emotional similarities between men and women far outweighed the differences were the most successful finding and attracting dates. . . . [the] major adjustment occurs when the divorced person stops thinking in sexual and social stereotypes.[22]

Emerging gracefully from the old self involves rediscovering one's creative center which is gradually being revealed in and through the stages of life. Jungian psychotherapists consistently articulate this belief that there is a unique sacred individuality to each person. They describe the life of a person as a process of "individuation," a gradual development of the individual self in and through the experiences of life. Individuation is a gradual transformation of what is unconscious to a conscious realization that one's individuality is a profound mystery. This realization involves a sense of what Jungians call a "transpersonal" center to identity. Carl Jung expresses this by saying that "individuality has an *a priori* unconscious existence."[23]

The gradual realization of my absolutely unique original center and its role in the universe is thus not an exercise in "self-love" but a realization that there is more to the nature of my individuality and my potential wholeness than I can consciously know, control, or understand at any one time. It involves accepting and not condemning those aspects of one's behavior and personality which may appear immature, dependent, or compulsive. To condemn oneself for earlier choices, failed marriages, or personal commitments does not facilitate the process of growth into greater wholeness. There is no such thing as an unforgivable mistake in life. Only an acceptance of that behavior and an effort to look at its unconscious sources can integrate it into the gradual developing whole.

The end of my marriage shattered my growing sense of complacency and pride at my own success. I was unmasked and that prideful girl was no more. Gradually, from the silence of the months of pain I began to talk to friends that I had cut off from seeing my anguish. At first I heard only my self-pity as I told the story of the failure of my hope. Gradually the immediate grief faded and I began to rebuild. I started to recognize my own complicity in our failure to risk or to trust communication. I discovered old and new friendships and the ability to learn trust again. The divorce aged me, it stripped me bare of my false pretenses of innocence and self-satisfaction. I recognized unconscious drives and motivations in myself as the result of the failure of that marriage. Maybe nothing has been more productive of growth in myself than what I initially experienced as a death.

The time of loss and failure may be a critical opportunity for a woman to bring into focus those aspects of herself that have remained unconscious, to discover new elements of the self that have been latent. There will need to be a healing, a movement from despair and self-condemnation into a rebirth of hope in a new self. In our society *therapy* offers the most common ritual for healing. Therapy can be helpful if it does not involve "adjustment to the situation." The possibility for a rebirth, for a graceful experience of the crisis, involves understanding the role that tragedy, evil, and suffering may play in forming the human personality. Trust in the renewing quality of life and one's gradual growth into a deeper level of self-understanding and wholeness presupposes a trust that one's life is a gift, a mystery, a personality that is always developing. Taking one's self ultimately seriously may be hard for many women in this culture because they have been taught that this is selfish. Self-acceptance and dedication to the uniquely creative center found in each individual is not selfishness. It is finally a sense of responsibility to the particular individual whose role in life is to express its creative power in as many forms as possible and bring the hidden potential into conscious expression.

Edward Edinger comments in *Ego and Archetype*:

> In my experience the basis of almost all psychological problems is an unsatisfactory relation to one's urge to individuality. And the healing process often involves an acceptance of what is commonly called selfish, power-seeking or autoerotic. The majority of patients in psychotherapy need to learn how to be more effectively selfish and more effective in the use of their own personal power; they need to accept responsibility for the fact of being centers of power and effectiveness. So-called selfish or egocentric behavior which expresses itself in demands made on others is not effective conscious self-centeredness or conscious individuality. We demand from others only what we fail to give ourselves. If we have insufficient self-love or self-prestige, our need expresses itself unconsciously by coercive tactics towards others. And often the coercion occurs under the guise of virtue, love or altruism. Such unconscious selfishness is ineffectual and destructive to oneself and to others. It fails to achieve its purpose because it is blind, without awareness of itself. What is required is not the extirpation of selfishness, which is impossible but rather that it be wedded to consciousness and thus becomes effective.[24]

Self-awareness and consciousness become the key to discovering one's individuality and being responsible to it. Knowledge is thus the precursor for a graceful experience of self-renewal. In this discussion of self-love, Edward Edinger is not particularly focusing upon women, but, in my opinion, self-love remains a basic problem for women. The image of identity prescribed for them has been so closely connected with "being for" another —lover, child, husband, parent, even a cause. Women have defined their existence in terms of being needed, and that is why the crisis of broken relationships so frequently involves a profound personal and spiritual dilemma for them. To realize that the primary responsibility in life is to our own individuality, what Jungians call our "selves," is a spiritual and not an egocentric commitment. It involves recognizing our unique individuality as a gift of the process of life. It is a form of ultimate self-acceptance and a sense of self-worth, akin to what Christianity has called being aware that we are justified by God. This sense of ultimate self-trust involves being aware of all the so-called undesirable elements of oneself—fears, loneliness, and guilt—and accepting them as part of the whole personality. Our unique personhood is thus a wondrous thing in process of unfolding.

Accepting one's particular individuality as unique involves trusting our *aloneness*, the essential separateness of ourselves from one another. Each of us has a particular destiny. We come into the world alone, and we die alone. Realizing our uniqueness involves a recognition that we cannot finally be dependent on any other person for our being. Emerging from a crisis we often see loneliness as the only promise. There is a distinction though between aloneness and loneliness, and we need to trust that through the negative experience of loneliness will emerge the positive experience of being alone. Being alone is a positive state, an understanding that we are unique, creative centers of life, essentially separate persons. Ultimately we cannot submerge our identity into others. Being alone is not loneliness; it is tragic in some respects, but it is also our opportunity for life and for expressing ourselves. The grace that we discover as we grow into this new sense of aloneness is that we are indeed related to others:

. . . at the center of the experience of individuality is the realization that all other individuals share the same experience as ourselves of living in a single, sealed world, and this realization connects us meaningfully with all other units of life. . . . We are *both* unique indivisible units of being and also part of the contiuum which is the universal wave of life.[25]

Until we recognize our uniqueness as individuals and believe in it, we will be unable to find a true sense of our identity with others. The paradox is that discovering the self comes only in and through interaction with others. As a child, one's personality, one's sense of individuality, emerges from the response of a loving environment, as Erikson documents in his discussion of the five stages of childhood.[26] Trusting interaction creates the possibility for developing a sense of the self, for self-love. In adulthood there is no escape from commitment, choice, sexual expression, vocation. Risk is a necessary element, and in that interaction, self-expression, and crisis, there will be gradual self-discovery and growth in individuality. Indeed experiences of loss, failure, guilt, and despair are necessary in order to facilitate the gradual realization of one's selfhood. Edinger comments that Jung discovered that the word for "individual" is etymologically related to the word *widow*.[27] Jung noted that in a Manichean text Jesus was called "the son of the widow."[28]

Widow means the parted one. Hence, prior to widowhood one is not yet an individual, indivisible, but is still subject to a parting process. The symbolism tells us that widowhood is an experience on the pathway to the realization of individuality, in fact, that individuality is the son of that experience. This can only mean that man must be parted from that on which he is dependent but which he is not, before he can become aware of that which he is, unique and indivisible.[29]

To emerge strengthened from an experience of loss and failure is to die and to be reborn. The descent into "hell," into loneliness and despair is the means to a new sense of individuality, a new trust in one's creative role in life. Many will not emerge from a such an experience transformed; they will not perceive the need to seek aids to healing and will escape into bitterness and despair. The destruction will be internalized rather than utilized as the means to new life. The spiritual question that the crisis raises is whether we can see it as an opportunity for a deepening sense of ourselves as individuals, a discovery of our own potential as female human beings, and an acceptance of the responsibility that each of us has to actualize our creative potential at each stage of existence.

6.

Marriage

Every Saturday afternoon in summer I sit on my front steps and watch the wedding parties go in and come out of the church across the street. The bride is veiled and pretty in white; several bridesmaids are elaborately dressed (hats are "in" this year), and the young men are awkward and hot in their rented color-coordinated tuxedos. The cars are covered with tissue pompoms in pink and white, and the bridal car roof is decorated with a huge tissue wedding bell or swan. Fifteen minutes after they arrive they are outside again, posing for pictures while the bride's mother and the photographer tell everyone where to stand. Then they are off in a shower of confetti and honking horns. As soon as they leave, the remnants of confetti are vacuumed up, and in thirty minutes the next lot arrive.

Is this what it amounts to? Is this the best we can do? Is this really all we can say about "the happiest day in a girl's life"? What happens in those few moments in church (and most of us still insist on being married in church) to symbolize the transition from two persons into a "married couple"? Whether we do it the old way and promise love and fidelity until death do us part, or the new way and promise commitment "while love shall last," we all go in there and swear before our family, friends, and God that we will create a new life and a home and will accept the responsibility of a family with this one man. We all *mean* what we say. Why then are so many disappointed in the reality of marriage and yet return again and again to promise those same things and search for that dream for once and for all?

Our weddings are out of joint. Particularly for the woman they fail to symbolize the nature of the transition. In a romantic haze of glory the wedding day is the bride's, her time of triumph in which she gives herself to the man she loves. It is a day of joy, beauty, and radiance. It marks the transformation of a "virgin" to a wife. In our culture weddings focus on the bride; all the fuss is for her, and the bridegroom plays a distinctively secondary role. On this day of happiness our tears are in joy although the bride's mother is permitted to weep at the thought of losing her daughter.

The wedding is the beginning of marriage, and it is the most important ritual event in the life of a woman in this culture. As a symbol of her new role in life, the mythology we associate with weddings fails radically, in my mind, to provide an adequate "rite of passage." The images and framework suggested in this cultural expression of "becoming a wife" are actually demonic, for they distort the meaning of marriage and the woman's implied role. The failure of marriages in our society is the failure of the myth of happiness and romantic love. The disappointment and psychological ill-health that women experience within marriage[1] begin at the wedding since this provides the symbolic reference point to which we return to find meaning for marriage and our roles within it.

Marriage is a crisis for men and for women. A marriage is an action involving oneself with another individual in a public, formal, legal, and personal bond. A marriage always involves a public statement of sexual commitment, sexual rights, and property rights and involves the issue of accepting responsibility for children born or adopted into the union. A marriage constitutes therefore a complex interrelationship between a personal, private commitment and a public role for the couple, accepted and validated by the community through the medical profession, the legal profession, and the financial establishment. A marriage gives to individuals rights and obligations toward the spouse and the progeny. A marriage is also a sacred event; some call it a "sacrament," an estate sanctified by God, an eternal framework within which children are to be raised and the partners are to find sexual expression, love, comfort, and mutual support.

In our culture marriage as a social institution reflects the inherited patriarchal pattern of the Judeo-Christian tradition and its concepts of the structural relation between male and female within marriage. The following statement from Ephesians has remained the accepted basis for marriage within a religious and secular context. "Wives, be subject to your husbands as to the Lord; for the man is the head of the woman, just as Christ also is the head of the church. Christ is, indeed, the Saviour of the body; but just as the church is subject to Christ, so must women be to their husbands in everything" (Eph. 5:23–24, NEB). Some writers can see no hope for the stability and future of society if the preeminent authority of the male is undermined.[2] It is said that the male must be the leader in the home due to his natural aggressive character and the essential dependence of women, for example in intercourse and in childbearing.[3]

The wedding service still carries symbols of this submission of the woman to the man. The custom of "giving away" the bride derives from the view that the woman was not her own mistress but the property of her father and then was transferred to become the property of her husband.[4] Likewise, the bridal veil is "unquestionably a symbol of submission."[5] In contemporary marriage liturgies there is often little overt reference to submission of the woman to the man; indeed the stress is on equal status of the two before God. Nevertheless, a couple becomes *man* and *wife*, and the basic structure of patriarchy is assumed: the woman will take his name and bear his children to carry on his line. The financial dependence of the woman and the children on the man is assumed in marriage as are the social obligations of the male to support the female and any progeny.

The attitude of women toward marriage has been different from that of men because of the implied social role that men and women have played in marriage. Judith Bardwick suggests that marriage represents something distinctive to men and to women.

Women have a choice between working and not working and men do not. But women do not have the psychological freedom of not marrying, while men (to some extent) do.[6]

The psychological, economic, sexual, and physical dependency that women have on marriage within a patriarchal framework means that getting married represents a personal and social achievement for the woman, whereas for the man "it belongs to his personal life."[7] Marriage for a woman therefore has represented, not merely one factor of her life among others, but *the* achievement, a "career" in itself, the foundation of her personal and social identity. Love is now the basis for marriage in our society, and women marry to prolong and deepen the romantic feelings that they experienced before marriage.[8] To marry, for a woman in this society, represents the fulfillment of her hopes for happiness. She has a man who loves her, she has a home, she can have children, she has someone to support her, she has emotional and financial security, and she has social status. While a young woman may contribute financially to the home, marriage represents the ability of the woman to be economically and emotionally dependent on the male and finally not to have to be responsible for supporting herself or the other. Marriage in that sense represents *the* decision of a woman's life; she moves into a state of being a wife and probably a mother, into a state of security and mature adulthood which nothing radically changes.[9] "Marriage is a state towards which young Americans are propelled, and within which American women, educated to be energetic and active, try to live out the desires that have been both encouraged and muffled in them as children."[10]

The tragedy of this attitude toward marriage on the part of women is that the expectation that being a wife and mother will answer the questions of identity has been found wanting. The value that our society places on a woman's fulfilling the traditional roles in marriage and in childbearing (in spite of the mythology) is so minimal that she finds neither the husband, the children, nor the home can provide a sense of security about her worth. Bardwick comments that marriage is the resolution of one identity crisis and the beginning of another.[11] Marriage in fact creates the need for the reassurance of love[12] and in several regards creates a deeper feeling of vulnerability in the woman. The sense of emptiness expressed by this twenty-five-year-old woman points to a lack of self-worth that many women find in marriage:

I've done everything women are supposed to do—gardening, hobbies, antiques, social teas with the neighbours, work for the hospital guild and participating in the local P.T.A. I can do it all, and to a point I enjoy it, but I still feel empty, with a big sense of nothing, when it is all over. I love my husband, I was never cut out to be a career woman, and I love my children, but inside I am discontented and desperate. I feel I have no personality, there is no me—who am I?[13]

The feelings expressed by this woman are reflected in the statistical analysis of the high incidence of married women's psychological distress.[14] Marriage literally makes women sick as they try to cope with the complex demands of being housewife, valet, mistress, mother, and often outside wage earner. Kathrin Perutz suggested that women are doomed to incompetence and a feeling of failure in their attempt to juggle all these expected roles.[15] The frustrations of women in traditional marriage roles are also due to the low status of housework, their social isolation in the home, and the gradual erosion of their confidence to deal with the "outside world."[16] Jessie Bernard quotes Alice Rossi to the effect that "the possibility must be faced . . . that women lose ground in personal development and self-esteem during the early and middle years of adulthood, whereas men gain ground in these respects during the same years."[17]

The attempt to find a total identity in a concept of oneself as primarily wife or mother leads to destructive effects, not only on the development and growth of the personality of the woman, but also ultimately on the husband and the children. It enhances the passive and dependent role of the woman in the relationship and encourages her to become a shrew. To ask another to carry the burden of financial responsibility and initiative is a form of passive manipulation. It places the male under a continual obligation to carry both the psychological and the emotional burdens of the marriage. Women often ask men to live out their dreams so that they can experience them vicariously.[18] While in any marriage there is initially a large degree of projecting the alienated aspect of the self onto the mate, unless the woman can move beyond allowing the mate to carry those qualities that she hopes one day to possess and can start to incorporate them into her own selfhood, she will begin to resent the partner for denying them to her.[19] Until a woman goes beyond this form of dependency, there can be no real relationship, and she can experience no real sense of identity. She will behave as a vengeful influence on those around her. "The negative role of bitch is almost built into woman's role and it surfaces at the heart of the duality of marriage if this is the only place where she has a chance to exercise power."[20]

The dangers surrounding getting married for a woman are great. She must battle with her internalized desires to be made happy ever after through getting married, and she must reckon with the destructive mythologies concerning the nature of marriage and the role of the woman within it that have been sanctified by church and society. Looking to marriage for her identity and internalizing the expected dependent role represent an overwhelming temptation and lead perhaps to deep unhappiness and almost certainly to a form of spiritual poverty. Finding the thread of her identity in and through the current structure of marriage is well-nigh impossible within the present patriarchal and sex-linked preconceptions of married roles. The romantic myth of the bride who gives herself totally to the man she loves, expecting the structure of being a wife to substitute for a continuing sense of responsibility for one's individuality, remains the most demonic form of the meaning of marriage for women. Unfortunately it is exceedingly difficult to find any other basis for self-understanding or for seeing the genuine possibilities for marriage as a graceful experience. The structure of marriage and the expectations that women have of marriage must change in order for them to find growth within it or indeed for the institution to survive at all. For marriage to survive

girls will have to learn that however large marriage may loom in their lives it is not nirvana, that it does not mark the end of their growth, that motherhood is going to be a relatively transient phase of their lives, that they cannot indulge themselves by investing all their emotional and intellectual resources in their children, that they cannot count on being supported all their lives simply because they are wives. They will have to prepare for loving autonomy rather than symbiosis or parasitism in marriage.[21]

The emotional and spiritual danger in which a woman stands as she enters marriage is enormous. Too many inner voices are leading her to expect essential fulfillment as a woman in being a wife. The religious tradition, the psychological tradition of the West, a woman's parents, and societal expectations and pressures teach her that marriage is essential to her fulfillment. In that marriage she gives up her individuality and her right to herself as she moves from being a virgin, either symbolically or literally, to becoming a wife and mother.[22] To find herself enhanced through marriage and not destroyed and to discover the graceful possibilities within the institution of marriage in this society represents one of the most fundamental of all spiritual challenges facing women today. She and her partner will need an ultimate sense of trust in themselves and in each other to realize that possibility.

The potential for a woman to experience marriage as graceful depends on the symbolic framework she uses to interpret the meaning of marriage and her identity in relation to it. The essential prerequisite for a creative marriage is her attitude toward herself as an individual, a woman having an autonomous journey in life. She must perceive a pattern of growth and uniqueness in herself that no particular role can embody although all relationships and functional roles contribute to that process of growth. A woman is a "virgin" as she enters marriage; in these days virginity is not so frequently technical as it is psychological. In order for women to discover grace in marriage they must indeed retain that psychological virginity. Esther Harding in *Women's Mysteries: Ancient and Modern* described the common characteristics of the Virgin Moon Goddesses present in many ancient religions such as the Greek goddess Demeter, the Egyptian goddess Isis, and the Christian image of the Virgin Mother. The quality of "virginity" that each of these goddesses had was not identical with sexual immaturity but defined an essential autonomy of spirit.

Harding described the virgin goddess in her relationship to other gods in this manner:

The God with whom she is associated is her son and him she necessarily precedes. Her divine power does not depend on her relation to a husband-god, and thus her actions are not dependent on the need to conciliate such a one or to accord with his qualities and attitudes. For she bears her own divinity in her own right.[23]

The essential "at-one-in-herself" characteristic of these Moon Goddesses is what I mean by psychological virginity. This virginity is maintained through all the functions of being in relation to a male, a lover, or a mother. She never becomes a "wife," that is, *defined by* her relationship to the male.[24]

The ability to retain this sense of virginity, to find the autonomy of spirit enhanced rather than destroyed by marriage, depends on the nature of a woman's resolution of the previous life-crises. If marriage represents psychological and physical movement from her father's house to her husband's house, she will play the same dependent role. She will look to her husband for self-affirmation and approval by being pleasing and coquettish like a daughter and by protecting him and sacrificing herself for him like a mother. In such a marriage she cannot encounter and respect the autonomy of the male since she has never "left home." She carries into marriage the need for self-affirmation and protection that she received from her parents. She also carries the attitudes, expectations, and values of her mother and father into the new situation and attempts to live her life by them. She has not been through the necessary separation from her parents, nor has she "died" to the state of childhood. She has not struggled to find a female identity distinct from her mother's. She has also not discovered a sense of herself and her unique inherent life-force which must recognize its own patterns and accept responsibility for its own value system.

The action of getting married represents therefore a death in oneself to the power of parents. A maturing marriage is not an escape from parental influence to a husband but a statement to oneself and the community that the process of leaving the parental home and every "home," physically and most importantly psychologically, that has already begun can now take public form. Marriage for a woman can then be an act of trust that the process of dying and being reborn in oneself may continue in and through intimate interaction with another in a formal establishment of a common home and a public role and an acceptance of responsibility for furthering the process of life biologically and spiritually in oneself and in relation to the other. The beginning of a marriage is an identity crisis for both individuals since it acknowledges the dying process in each partner. Too often that dying has been seen by the woman as the death of herself so that she can now live for the man. Rather, an enriching marriage acknowledges that the process of dying and being born in oneself already begun can be witnessed and aided by the presence of the other. It cannot be done by the other; no person can live your life for you, but it can be shared and fostered by the other through the process of interaction and the grace of time.

The promises of the wedding service are not an acknowledgment by the woman or the man that personal wholeness is now achieved, that one is now ready to be in relation. The act of being married is an act of faith in the present and in the future. It professes trust in full understanding that the growth toward

personal maturity and wholeness involving many stages of discovery may now continue and be fostered by the interaction of
the other. It accepts the other in his or her wholeness in the
present and in his or her growth into the future. The pledge in
the marriage service is the partners' promise to be spiritually
whole for each other, *really* present, that their full individuality
in all its despicable and admirable qualities will be made
known. To promise this is an act of deep courage, for it involves
unmasking, not only to oneself in the secret of one's heart, but
to one who in many respects will always remain a stranger. The
fears surrounding the promises of marriage are that the potential for wholeness in each partner may never be realized and
that the closeness of the other will deepen the mistrust of that
process of self-revelation. Luckily in those fears one is not alone
but with another human being who equally fears the processes
of dying and being reborn and of allowing another to see that
growth.

In such a marriage there can be no roles prescribed by social
custom, nor can maleness and femaleness be interpreted stereo-
typically. The essential equality of the two persons in the relationship does not destroy the particular quality of each as man
and woman; it can only enhance it. Deane Ferm writes:

*Responsible sexuality will remain a pipe dream until mankind takes
seriously the conviction that men and women are to be treated as
equals. Only then will society understand the radical changes that
must take place in the structure of marriage and the family. The
objective is not to destroy monogamous marriage and the family,
but rather, to destroy the conditions within these institutions which
have placed women in an inferior role.*[25]

Interpreting one's identity within marriage as male and female
must involve accepting the biological character of each and yet
disavowing the traditional categories of masculinity and feminity that we have used to interpret sexual distinction.

When husbands and wives strictly adhere to separate, completely
distinct roles, true understanding between them becomes virtually

impossible. By sharing and exchanging roles, that understanding can be achieved, and with it, a new closeness and intimacy.[26]

The O'Neills' concept of an "open marriage" shares this view that the possibility for growth in each partner depends on destroying the notion of a "couple-front"[27] and accepting the unique individuality of both the man and the woman in the relationship. The only possibility for seeing that individuality lies in recognizing that our common humanity transcends maleness and femaleness. To remain locked into a narrow interpretation of appropriate roles will lead finally, to the increasing diminution, not only of the individuals, but of their ability to trust in the other. "Equality, then, is based upon personhood, upon the sense of individual identity that is developed when both partners in a marriage grant one another privacy, open companionship, and freedom from stipulated roles."[28]

Marriage in itself cannot bring a woman identity, security, love, or purpose in life, nor can it fulfill her dreams. Sense of fulfillment in the context of a marriage relationship comes not *from* the marriage but from the actively growing lives that witness in pleasure and awe the development of the other into his or her potential.

Open marriage is looking at your life together as a co-operative venture, in which the needs of each can be fulfilled without an overriding dependency that cripples the other's self-expression. Love can then be understood as a sharing of one another's independent growth rather than as a possessive curtailment of growth.[29]

The O'Neills expressed hope that such a marriage would entail the acceptance of sexual freedoms outside the marriage. In my view, this expectation underestimates the nature of trust possible within such a concept of open marriage. When marriage involves such an open trust and self-understanding, the search for sexual fulfillment outside that relationship becomes unnecessary. All forms of sexual feelings and desires can be acknowledged both to the self and to the other so that they may be integrated into the continuing process of self-discovery. To seek sexual fulfillment outside an open marriage can lead ultimately, not to increased self-trust and openness, but to a lack of faith in the other to accept and enhance the sexual relationship between them. A marriage of openness necessarily implies fidelity, not because the love is possessive and jealous, but because the love is freely given and the trusting complete. In that trust there is no need to turn to another for fulfillment of erotic desire since all compulsive and hidden feelings, heterosexual or homosexual, may be brought into the context of the relationship and accepted both by the self and the other.

Do women then *need* marriage for their continuing search for selfhood? I believe that men and women do *need* each other, *not* because they represent opposite ends of the qualities of humanness and not to complete (so briefly) a biological moment called procreation, but because they can learn from each other. In this statement I commit myself to a view that the shared experience of being human is affected by body space and distinctive physical and emotional experiences connected with those events. Regardless of the particular cultural interpretation given to menstruation, pregnancy and childbirth, lactation, and menopause, these events *are* part of my psychosomatic unity as a woman. A male, who can never experience his own body from these points of view, *needs* to learn from me as a woman what these particular experiences can teach us both about the mystery of life and death. I as a woman, in encountering a male in his psychosomatic unity, will not only learn the distinctive nature of male sexuality and how it can teach us both about the life process, I will also encounter him as he struggles to interpret his male identity in relation to a sense of ultimate meaning.

The willingness to enter into a relationship of trust and mutuality with one who is and must remain in some essential ways a stranger marks the difference between the heterosexual and the homosexual relationship. In the essential otherness of the partner there may be an opportunity for a form of growth for an enhanced sense of one's individuality as male or female, and for new self-understanding. Perhaps this is what causes many primitive communities to depict marriage as a ritual androgynization.[30] This use of intersexual transvestism as a wedding custom may appear strange to us; yet in marriage we take on the sexuality of the other. Jungian psychotherapists have commented that the true nature of love is hermaphroditic.[31] James Hillmann in his *Myth of Analysis* comments that "approximation to the hermaphrodite is a death experience; the movement into death proceeds through bisexuality."[32]

Marriage therefore can represent the willingness of a woman to find in herself an openness to and an understanding of the particular elements of male experience that are also part of woman's life, psychologically if not biologically. For a man to marry a woman represents his opportunity to see her femaleness, not as other and unavailable to him, but as part of his own essential humanness. The growth toward wholeness in personal development may thus be toward an "androgynous" consciousness,[33] a state in which we see the opposite sex, not as fundamentally alien and opposite from oneself, but as woven into the fabric of one's being. Marriage offers men and women the time and the trust to know and reintegrate the hidden aspects of the self through encounter with the other's sexuality. Unfortunately, too often the marriage is expected to provide security and reaffirmation of the traditional male and female forms of behavior and self-understanding, and so the opportunity is missed.

The crisis of marriage which begins as soon as the vows are made is not primarily "adjusting" to the needs of the spouse and the new roles of "being a wife" or "being a husband." It is rather the beginning of a crisis of self-discovery. *Every* element of one's personality will be revealed. Each nasty, snivelling, jealous, prejudicial, fearful, ungrateful, vain, insecure, hostile emotion in oneself will be made known in the act of relating to the other. All the unkindness, cowardice, and greed of the other will also be made known. The temptations of marriage will be to identify the confidence, security, wisdom, and the maleness with the other and to find none in oneself, *or* to identify the destructive aspects of personality totally with the other and to find none present in oneself.

There are times when I play the "feminine" role, when it
suits me. How easy those conventions are to fall into! "Allow-
ing" Dan to fill the car at a self-service gas station in the middle
of Winnipeg winter is a typical example of my "feminine" be-
havior. Why I as the "wife" should presume the privilege of not
getting out into the snow and cold, has never been questioned.
Ah, liberation can be a drag, self-awareness brings the painful
knowledge of my own duplicity!

The opportunity for spiritual growth within marriage rests on
being able to overcome this alienation—categorizing roles and
behavior into "feminine and masculine"[34] and alienating
within oneself "acceptable" and "unacceptable" aspects of the
personality. The all-pervading, ever-seeing presence of the other
is both the possibility and the fear in this journey of self-discovery. In the lived reality of the relationship the other becomes
the mirror by which the process of unmasking may take place.
It is a stripping into nakedness, symbolically and literally. In
that vulnerability lies also the possibility for new growth and a
deeper sense of self-acccptance. The reciprocity of seeing and
being seen and of finding at that point of spiritual nakedness
affirmation and not condemnation, hope and not despair, *is* the
grace that a married relationship may bring. It is repeatedly
necessary to put faith in the process of growth into strength and
self-trust through the power of the relationship. For many days
it may seem that growth has ceased and that the other has
withdrawn. And then an event, a shared moment of joy or
sorrow, of personal triumph or common despair, will bring
forth again a mutual sense of awe, wonder, and the mystery of
life in which both partners find themselves reaffirmed in their
total individuality in and through the presence and support of
the other.

There are days in our marriage when the closeness of our
lives breaks through to a new level. There are days when I risk
self-disclosure and show you my anxieties, my anger, my fears.
In that risking I have been met by you with acceptance and
sharing. I have felt very close to you. We are open to one

another at that moment. These are the times that I treasure as the joy of our marriage. There are days when I forget and become afraid of trusting my vulnerability. As I risk again I discover that you are there, wrestling with your own fears, and we find new strength in each other.

These are moments of grace; they cannot be programmed, and when they come, they may leave us speechless. In these moments new understanding may be gained of the promise made at weddings that this relationship may be "forever" or "until death do us part." In face of these moments there is nothing to fear, nothing at all. The promise at the beginning of marriage is a statement of hope that the common process of growth may begin and that the other may be a witness and aid to that journey. A wedding does not *make* people married. Marriage itself is not a state or a new identity one achieves on a certain day. Marriage is rather a possibility, a potential, a hoped-for reality begun on a certain day but unrealized for many years. Marriage itself *is* the process through which the individuals within it gradually achieve ever-deepening forms of self-acceptance and personal growth through daily interaction. The hoped-for moments of grace which reveal to the partners their common commitment are symbolic occasions that provide the two with a shared understanding of the meaning of life, the uniqueness of their individualities, and the singular value of their mutual bond.

The act of marrying for a woman is then a crisis that continues. The dangers of formulating a restrictive understanding of marriage and identity within it and of looking to marriage for a false identity are very real. The rituals that our culture uses to symbolize the nature of marriage fail to articulate a proper view of the necessary death and rebirth and the graceful possibilities of that relationship and of growth within it. No other event involves a woman in such a great risk since it is within the context of that relationship that the experience of her female sexuality in pregnancy and childbirth may be carried out and the further life-crises of parenthood, maturity, and old age must be negotiated. The hope for a marriage is that it may provide, not only a context for increased personal trust and growth and self-understanding, but that it may in itself be creative in its power to reveal a sense of the mystery of life, our aloneness and togetherness in face of it, and the continual element of dying and being reborn that constitutes the very wonder of it all.

7.

Pregnancy and Birth

I was quite anxious about my pregnancy. I was so tired at the beginning and used to fear that I would miscarry. During that first winter of my pregnancy I walked with great care. I was terrified of slipping on the ice and falling. During the last month of pregnancy my husband and I were out in the car. He started to drive rather fast. I eventually expressed my growing sense of discomfort. My hands were sweating and I was very frightened. Suddenly I had no ability to cope with speed and he was searching for freedom and release by driving through the night. He was very angry at me, I was emotional and fearful. As we drove slowly home in silence I was aware how the new shape of my body had changed my sense of spatial relationships. I wanted to protect the baby from potential harm. I was experiencing myself and my body in a way neither I nor my husband could clearly understand.

Perhaps no change in a woman's life is more radical than the experience of being pregnant and giving birth. It is a relatively short experience in terms of time, and though it may be repeated, each pregnancy raises the question of a woman's self-understanding in a new way. Pregnancy and birth involve an identity crisis for a woman. She is challenged to formulate a new self-concept, a new understanding of herself in relation to her physiology, and a new view of the meaning of her fertility. Pregnancy and birth challenge not only the woman's sense of herself as an individual but also her relationship to the father of the child and her anticipated relationship with the baby as its mother. Fundamentally, pregnancy and birth locate a woman in an experience of the body and a perception of the self that is uniquely female. That uniqueness can bring both pride and fear; it links her unalterably with those who have experienced pregnancy and childbirth and separates her from those who will never experience it.

Pregnancy and childbirth is a spiritual crisis for a woman, not only in the sense that it raises questions about the interpretation of her femaleness, but also because it implies making a decision about the meaning of the creative power of fertility. The personal experience of this dramatic change in one's body, through which new life is harbored and expelled, is a "sacred" event. The questions of the meaning of the whole and an understanding of life and death are vividly presented to the individual woman and the community. Pregnancy and birth are indeed times of danger, a limited physiological danger these days, but a more radical spiritual and psychological danger for the woman. There *is* the opportunity for the graceful experience of pregnancy and birth whereby the event can be integrated into a new self-concept and sense of personal meaning in relation to a perspective on life. The demonic possibility is also present whereby the crisis character of the event is ignored, or the fears are intensely magnified, so that the woman finds herself unable to accept the processes happening to her and sees the experience as overwhelmingly negative and destructive of her self-identity.

The spiritual and psychological dangers inherent in the experience of pregnancy and birth exist, not only because it puts a woman as close to death as it does to life, but also because these events happen *through* her. She does not appear in control of her body although her attitude towards her body affects how she experiences the events. The ability to relax into accepting the dramatic and often unknown changes in her body are harder in this culture perhaps than in earlier times because we assume that the mind *controls* the body. Margaret Mead's comments about the nature of female body rhythms are no more appropriate than in reference to the time of pregnancy and birth.

Coming to terms with the rhythms of women's lives means coming to terms with life itself, accepting the imperatives of the body rather than the imperatives of an artificial, man-made, perhaps transcendentally beautiful civilization. Emphasis on the male work-rhythm is an emphasis on infinite possibilities; emphasis on the female rhythms is an emphasis on a defined pattern, on limitation.[1]

This experience of being limited by a process that has its own innate structure and timing poses one of the deepest challenges to personal identity. Even when the pregnancy is planned and long-desired, the experience of gestation and, even more critically, the actual labor and birth involve an individual woman's being caught up in a movement that is *not* personal, that affects her feelings, her shape, her total self. To experience dread at the beginning of pregnancy or toward the end is an appropriate response to a process that has its own intentionality and is essentially *impersonal.* Ambiguous feelings about pregnancy and birth are initially connected with this sense of being determined, not being in control. The feelings of fear, resentment, and hostility to having become part of this ongoing process are not something of which women should be ashamed; they are a real response to the implications of that experience which presents a radical challenge to self-identity. "A woman should realize that the very intensity of her fear may be related to her positive feelings, to her sense that she is charged with something extremely valuable."[2]

Arthur and Libby Colman's discussion of pregnancy includes a recognition that it represents an identity crisis, offering to the woman a possibility for the formulation of a new identity. In their studies they discovered that women feel there is something wrong in having feelings of terror during pregnancy.[3] The increased anxiety of the pregnant woman may be intensified by feeling guilty for experiencing something that "should be" wonderful as fearful and threatening to her traditional self-concept.

Pregnant women, as well as postpartum women, not only need more physiological information about their body processes, they also need an acceptance by society and by the medical profession that pregnancy and birth are crisis times. Denying negative feelings by facile reassurance or medical information ignores the woman's need to articulate her feelings in some symbolic form and to proceed through the dark aspects of the experience into a new form of self-understanding. The medical profession and its attitude toward the woman, her husband, and the experience of birth largely determines the modern rituals observed concerning pregnancy and birth. Since the experience is no longer so dangerous for the woman in Western society and the mortality rate for infants has been significantly lowered by the advent of pre-natal care and modern medical methods, it is easy to ignore the fears and anxieties. Pregnancy and birth *can* be an opportunity in personal growth *if* the crisis character of the event is not ignored. The Colmans' suggest that

pregnancy is neither a static nor a brief experience, but one full of growth, change and enrichment. It is a time when one's life impinges directly on the most basic psychological and physiological processes, when abstractions like fertility, fulfillment and death become of more immediate and personal concern.[4]

Pregnancy and birth, like every other life-crisis, involve a death, indeed a double death. At the beginning of pregnancy there is a death to the old prepregnant "virginal" self in order to allow the new entity of the developing fetus the space to grow. There is another death of the self in the process of birth, an end to the internal relationship of fetus and mother and a beginning of an external relationship between infant and mother. The theme of death itself is very real to a woman during pregnancy and involves not only her symbolic death and rebirth but also the very real fears of death of the fetus in a miscarriage or her own death during the birth.[5] The fact that few women die in childbirth does not alter this fear; giving birth is as close to dying as any other human experience. In it the forces of nature take over and make one insignificant in their power to deliver sorrow and joy. Preoccupation with death is not an irrational response to the anticipation or to the experience of birth. Birth and death are close together, and in giving birth a woman may learn more about death than in any other experience.

It is as though, by being closer to birth, to the beginning of life, these women were automatically closer to death. . . . pregnant women are more in touch with their entire life cycles than at any other times in their lives.[6]

The inability of this society to acknowledge the fearful elements of pregnancy and birth intensifies the natural ambiguity of the experience for women. Primitive societies understand the necessary ambiguous quality of this event and provided symbolic means whereby the individual and the community could experience the destructive elements of the event and be reborn with the new birth. For this reason the experience of childbirth has been surrounded by many taboos similar to menstrual taboos. In most societies these taboos took the form of secluding the mother during birth and for a period thereafter. Men and particularly a new mother's husband were not to touch her. In many cases her contact with food was restricted. She was to be fed by another, and food was handed to her at the end of a long stick.[7] The seclusion of the woman during and after childbirth and the fear of her potentially polluting effect strike us today as a cruel and inhuman manifestation of a lack of understanding concerning the processes of female sexuality. These rites, however, represent more than men's fear of female sexuality or their insecurity in face of something that was seen as a female power.[8] The fact that taboos arise and have similar functions in relation to other than female sexual events indicates that the taboos surrounding childbirth reflected a view that this event was sacred and to be handled with extreme care. Frazer suggests that the restrictions of touching herself imposed on menstruous and lying-in women were also imposed upon young men during puberty rites, for example, the Creek Indians.[9] Childbirth was seen as a particularly "dangerous" religious event both for the woman and for the community. The restrictions on the social contact of a woman who had miscarried or had been delivered of a still-born child were even more extreme.[10]

The seclusion of the woman indicates that the experience of childbirth was seen as dangerous for her too. The initiation rites for girls, called the *Chisungu*, described by Audrey Richards, reflect this need to remove the danger of menstruation, intercourse, and childbirth for a woman.[11] There was a "general fear of the birth of a child to a girl who has not received the magic protection given her by the chisungu rite."[12] In this case women were considered totally responsible for forming the child in the womb, and in many early cultures the male's role in procreation was not understood. The significant response of the tribe to the event of childbirth was that it was a *sacred* event, *mana*, involving great dangers and great possibilities for the beneficial effect of the power of fertility on the life of the tribe. For the woman, it was an event of spiritual danger. The rituals of seclusion and of "purification" after the lying-in period indicate that childbirth was an ordeal, a period of physical and spiritual crisis. The "churching of women" which still survives in the Episcopal church is a remnant of this purification rite: the need for a ritual to allow the death of the old self through the ordeal and transformation into a new state. The rites reflect the belief that the danger needs to be removed symbolically in order for the woman to pass unharmed into a new life.[13]

The common-sense attitude of our modern culture, in its desire to escape the destructive effects of ignorance and fear obvious in primitive superstitions, has ignored the beneficial psychological effects of an open acknowledgment and symbolic expression of the fears and dangers of pregnancy and childbirth. Modern obstetrics concentrates on removing anxiety by rational means and by stressing the "facts." For example Gordon Bourne in *Pregnancy* writes, "The emotional distress which may accompany pregnancy, labour and the puerperium is nearly always the result of ignorance."[14] He suggests that "it cannot be too strongly stressed that confidence comes directly from knowledge, and confidence in your ability comes from knowledge and reassurance."[15]

The stress on the need for information and for understanding processes of pregnancy and birth both for the mother and for the father, while an essential ingredient in developing a trusting attitude toward the body and this crucial experience of female sexuality, does not, in my mind, recognize that the physical and emotional changes of pregnancy and birth, while physiologically explainable, demand a new form of self-understanding on the part of the woman. She needs to come to terms with a new relationship to her sexuality and to others.

The anxieties associated with pregnancy and birth are partially connected with the physical change and some danger. The common statement today that taking the pill or having an abortion is less dangerous than becoming pregnant suggests that the natural experience of pregnancy and birth does involve risks both for the mother and for the child. While 97 percent of babies born may be perfectly normal,[16] a valid fear accompanies waiting for the unknown. One may not *presume* that the child will be normal. Pregnancy and birth also involve *real* physical discomforts. The modern stress on the ability of the mother to control the amount of pain she experiences during labor through relaxation, breath control, and education of her attitude toward her role in the birth process suffers sometimes from oversimplifying the nature of the experience.[17] Pregnancy and birth *do* involve physical and psychological changes that are intense, sometimes painful, and often frightening. The normality of these changes and our need to understand them fully should not blind us to the fact that pregnancy and birth are indeed a life-crisis for a woman because she must come to terms with the fears as well as the joys and attain a new understanding of herself.

Being able to experience pregnancy and birth as graceful depends on being able to express the fears and anxieties. Integrating the totality of the experience of pregnancy and birth lies in the ability to feel free to wrestle with the resentment and the ambiguity toward the fetus that being pregnant brings. Feelings of anxiety for the fetus or for oneself and the anticipated changes in personal style and freedom are important expressions of the mixed feelings for the dependent fetus and the soon-to-be dependent child. We must accept these reactions, not as "irrational," but as signs of the "ordeal," the crisis of identity. To emerge gracefully from the depths into a positive new self-concept and acceptance, a woman needs to recognize and articulate the crisis character of the events. In our society the medical profession concentrates primarily on the body. There are few community structures within which these feelings can be accepted and expressed.

In this light, statements concerning the experience of the fetus as a parasite on the woman can best be accepted as genuine feelings. Women feel hostile toward the life growing in them, *demanding* a response to its existence. Simone de Beauvoir's very negative interpretation of pregnancy for the life of a woman reflects a valid feeling that these bodily processes are ambiguous experiences:

. . . pregnancy is above all a drama that is acted out within the woman herself. She feels it as at once an enrichment and an injury; the fetus is a part of her body and it is a parasite that feeds on it; she possesses it, and she is possessed by it; it represents the future and carrying it, she feels herself vast as the world; but this very opulence annihilates her, she feels that she herself is no longer anything. A new life is going to manifest itself and justify its own separate existence, she is proud of it; but she also feels herself tossed and driven, the plaything of obscure forces.[18]

De Beauvoir's sense of the woman's passive role in pregnancy and childbirth reflects the quality of the identity crisis. The inevitably of the process, its impersonality, and the experience of being "fed upon," both during pregnancy and later during nursing, raise the question of the woman's individuality, her personal identity and powers, her creative influence upon the process. De Beauvoir concludes that "she does not really make the baby, it makes itself within her; her flesh engenders only flesh and she is quite incapable of establishing an existence that will have to establish itself."[19]

De Beauvoir's reaction to the ambiguity of pregnancy and birth is to despair. She sees no value in a role for the individual woman that she describes as innately dependent. Gestation for her is "a strange kind of creation which is accomplished in a contingent and passive manner."[20] In recording the ambiguity, the fears, and the feelings of personal alienation, de Beauvoir, unfortunately, never emerges from the demonic. She sees the passive role as inherently destructive of the individual and finds no way to integrate these crucial aspects of female sexuality into a new sense of identity. To be consumed by the despair leaves a woman divided in herself, resentful and angry at her biology. To fail to experience anything graceful in the processes of female sexuality and to emerge from the experience finally with bitterness constitute a demonic resolution of the crisis. There is no transformation for the woman; there is no new sense of selfhood.

Another form of demonic distortion of the experience of pregnancy and birth comes from an overidealization of it and from a romantic vision that a woman is *essentially* herself while pregnant. This vision sees an individual woman completely fulfilled in the collective role of life-giving. M. Esther Harding expresses this in her statement that

in pregnancy a woman attains biologically and psychologically, to the completeness of the Virgin Mother Goddess. . . . The pregnant woman has been worshipped from antiquity as representing something "in herself," something individual. Paradoxically, this aspect of individuality is attained through completely fulfilling a collective role; a pregnant woman is no longer what she has been—the embodiment of the personal—she is one of "The Mothers."[21]

The theory that a woman's personal identity is fulfilled in and through her identification with the collective role of the sacred life-giving power of the female may have been appropriate for antiquity, but it fails to appreciate the lack of symbolic female models in this society. We no longer worship the great goddess or see female procreativity as an expression of the goodness of the powers of life. A woman's identity may not be found any longer in this sacred role and responsibility since we no longer see it as a uniquely creative female power. The spiritual crisis of the woman in pregnancy and birth may not be solved by identifying with the symbol of the ancient "Great Mother Goddess." We need indeed to integrate the experience of female sexuality in pregnancy and birth into a *new* self-image. To see a woman's basic identity as fulfilled in childbearing and to condemn women who are humiliated or repulsed by this reduction as "superficial and egotistic"[22] represents, in my mind, a failure to appreciate the woman's necessary process of transformation *through* the ambiguity of the experience or the meaning of the woman's spiritual crisis of identity within the present cultural context. To find one's identity in being pregnant and giving birth, if it represents an individual woman's appropriating for her sense of herself a transcendent power and role, may indeed distort the meaning of selfhood.

Rollo May in his book *Love and Will* discusses the apparent discrepancy between the availability of birth control in modern society and the increase in the incidence of illegitimate pregnancies. He suggests that women in this society often struggle to prove their identity and personal worth through becoming pregnant and having a child. In a society where people feel alienated from themselves, depersonalized, and unable to *feel*, "we have forgotten that a girl can *yearn* to procreate, and can do so not just for psychobiological reasons but to break up the arid desert of feelingless existence."[23] Rollo May concludes that women often become pregnant in order to break through their feelings of lack of self-worth and lack of connectedness with the other and their own sexuality.

To search for an identity through becoming pregnant and bearing a child can be self-defeating for a woman because no child can supply the love and sense of self-worth she is seeking. A woman can also use pregnancy as an excuse to remain dependent and protected.[24] Being pregnant gives her a dominant status in a group; it draws attention to her and brings her privileges. For her to regard this attention as a sign of her worth as an individual and to seek to prove herself as an individual through her pregnancies represent, in my mind, demonic distortions of the possibilities that pregnancies and birth *do* offer for an enhanced sense of identity. This idealization of the pregnant woman is recorded by Havelock Ellis:

The whole carriage of the woman tends to become changed with the development of the mighty seed of man planted within her. . . . The pregnant woman has been lifted above the level of ordinary humanity to become the casket of an inestimable jewel.[25]

For an individual woman to look to pregnancy and birth to lift her above "the level of common humanity" to a transcendent status and identify herself with an "ideal figure" may render her unable to deal with the negative aspects of the experience. The actual birth can lead then to an increased sense of emptiness and deprivation. Likewise women who look to pregnancy and birth in order to prove themselves as individuals may experience deep emotional distress on having a miscarriage or on learning that they are unable to conceive. Sheila Kitzinger comments that some women are unable to reach orgasm after they learn it is impossible for them to have a child.[26]

Investing too much of one's identity as a woman into the ability to become pregnant and bear children can be as demonic as not investing enough, that is, *not* being able to integrate the changes in the body to a new sense of selfhood. Germaine Greer's comment that "childbearing was never intended by biology as a compensation for neglecting all other forms of fulfilment and achievement"[27] reflects our cultural situation. Biology itself intends nothing personal; it is what it is and follows its own laws. In our ability to control our biological potential for procreation we now are faced with a decision about its role in our continuing search for selfhood. We can choose never to become pregnant; we can hope to become pregnant once or twice or many times; we may never become pregnant and yet desire it. Our biology limits us. By itself it cannot provide the answer to the question of personal meaning. As Margaret Mead suggests, in primitive societies where the life span of women is shorter and female fertility is linked to a sacred power, there is no crisis over female identity, and a woman is sure of herself and her instinctive role.[28] In modern societies, however, a woman must *consciously* come to terms with the meaning of her pregnancy.[29] In wrestling with the joys and fears of the process she may indeed integrate them into a deeper understanding of herself and her female sexuality.

The woman with a firmly established sense of herself can best integrate the ambiguities of the experience into her continuing growth. "If a woman has never experienced a sense of *completeness* and firmly established identity—of being herself and content *in* herself—pregnancy may prove an acute threat to her self-image in just this way."[30] Studies have shown that women who have a very poor sense of themselves and little self-love and confidence will sense overwhelming anxiety in pregnancy and will experience continuing hostility to the fetus. This is the result of a severe hostility and rejection of the self.[31]

The possibilities that pregnancy and birth offer for new growth in the personality of the individual woman and for a self-enhancing experience of her biological processes depend therefore on self-love and an attitude of trust and acceptance toward the body. The resolution of the previous crises of female identity, the interpretation of sexuality in menstruation and sexual experience, and the establishment of a sense of self-worth will determine whether pregnancy and birth may be experienced gracefully or demonically. While the end of the process provides the impetus for becoming pregnant, namely the desire for a child, the experience itself offers a woman the possibility of participating in the actions of her body, not as burdens to be undergone, but as graceful experiences in their own right.

Pregnancy has three distinct psychological stages, each defined by certain physiological and psychological characteristics and by particular limits and potential for anxiety and enjoyment. The first stage, the first trimester, is dually ambivalent and joyful. The physiological effects during this period may be distinctly uncomfortable or minimal, apart from tiredness. The continuing discussion on the cause of morning sickness and whether it is primarily effected by hormonal changes or psychological factors is as yet unsolved. Many psychologists following Freud consider it a sign of symbolic rejection of the child, an "oral form of abortion."[32] Modern studies are showing that it is increasingly difficult to isolate the purely hormonal influences from the psychological factors influencing the emotions. Julia Sherman concludes:

The data . . . are remarkable in the extent to which they document the mutual influence of mind and body. In contrast, the role of pregnancy rejection and secondary gain in producing nausea or vomiting during pregnancy appears to have been exaggerated.[33]

Whether nausea and vomiting are caused primarily by hormonal factors[34] or by the "inner struggle of contradictory tendencies,"[35] it is evident that the whole experience of pregnancy presents a woman with a particularly close relation between the pleasant and unpleasant changes in her body and emotions. She is reminded forcibly of the psychosomatic unity of human existence. In pregnancy women experience what is often described as a state of "emotional lability." Psychiatrists have sometimes interpreted it as a stage of "instability." In one report a "great number" of prenatal cases were first diagnosed as borderline psychotic states and were later felt to be conditions peculiarly related to the crisis and disequilibrium unique to pregnancy![36] The tendency to regard the shifting emotional feelings common to pregnancy as potentially schizophrenic or for a woman to regard her emotional changes as neurotic is particularly unhelpful for finding an ability to accept and express the changes in mood as well as the changes in body awareness. The Colmans describe this increased "emotional lability," not as a time of excessive vulnerability and dependency, but rather as a time when a woman has an "altered state of consciousness."

Studies of pregnant women have shown that they were far more open, more willing to spill forth dreams, fantasies, anxieties and pleasures—all highly personal—than normal individuals in a non-pregnant state.[37]

The ability to find a context in which these feelings can be expressed remains a crucial task and need for the woman.

In a woman's first pregnancy, struggling with her anticipated new identity as a mother also involves redefining her identity in relation to the model of the female role offered by her mother. The Colmans suggest that one of the woman's important psychological tasks during the first months of pregnancy is to deal with her feelings of love, hate, frustration toward her mother. Finding a personally relevant mothering identity, separate and apart from that of her own mother, represents a significant aspect of the reordering of self-identity demanded by pregnancy.

The way in which a woman copes with this problem is critical to her future feelings about herself as a woman and mother and has far-reaching effects on her subsequent adjustments to pregnancy and motherhood.[38]

Pregnancy offers a woman the chance to wrestle with her relation to her mother, her identity with her, and her distinctiveness from her. It is a chance to find a unique style, a new perspective on herself as a woman in her procreative role. At the same time, it offers an opportunity, not only for increased self-understanding, but for an understanding of a human potential which is unique to women. The ability to know in her own body the processes of pregnancy and birth may give her a deeper perception of the particular feelings of women concerning their experience of the power of fertility working in and through them.

The second trimester of pregnancy is often described as one of greatest fulfillment and drive. The initial ambivalences have been resolved, and the visible evidence and gradual movement of the fetus can bring an increased sense of well-being, joy, energy, and self-confidence. An increased sense of her sexuality and new involvement with her husband are common for women during this stage.[39] The kicking of the baby in the womb is a positive experience, a sign of the woman's ability to experience the gradual growth of life in her body. At each stage of pregnancy, but particularly during the middle and the end, the issue of trust is clearly the focus of a woman's attention. The need to share feelings and anxieties with her husband and her doctor and friends is essential. A woman *is* dependent on others at the time of birth and before. Coming to terms with one's fears of trusting, voicing feelings, and making demands on others may be difficult for many women.[40] In relation to her husband or doctor, the distinctiveness of the female body experience may cause a woman to distrust her ability to articulate needs. Trust and faith in others is an essential prerequisite for the graceful experience of pregnancy and birth. In this experience of female sexuality as in others, knowledge of the physiological processes is a fundamental ingredient for trusting one's body and the changes happening to it.

The final trimester of pregnancy is often characterized by increased anticipation, joy, and anxiety. The crisis for a woman's identity focuses upon the process of birth itself and on her ability to cope with the child once it is born. Pain, fear of the unknown, loss of control, the sense that the baby may arrive at any moment, the pounding of the child on the inner organs and the abdomen, fears of the vulnerability of her body, and the need to protect the fetus all affect the anticipation of the birth. The joy that the birth is near also brings anxiety. At this stage the woman's attitude toward the birth and her ability to trust the processes of her body become essential for her anticipation of the experience of birth as well as her actual experience of it. The various methods of training for natural childbirth, helping a woman relax into the physical effort of labor and delivery, share a common perspective: the woman learns to trust, to cooperate with her body; she does not fear it or fight it. She understands the process and knows how to participate actively in the natural rhythms of the body. "To achieve the rhythmic coordination and harmony which is the essence of a beautifully controlled labour she must above all, *have learned to trust her body and her instincts.*"[41]

The physiological process of labor and delivery is affected by the attitude of the woman toward her body in general and by her trust in her sexuality and feelings. Sheila Kitzinger suggests that prolonged labors (over twenty-four hours) were found to come from mothers who were inhibited by what was happening to them, extremely ladylike, and unable to express their anxieties, though they suffered stoically.[42]

Giving birth involves an enormous amount of trust in the people around, in the body, and in the ability to allow the body to do its work. While proper preparation, psychologically and physically, for the event of birth through breathing techniques and relaxation exercises are most important, nothing contributes more to the graceful experience of labor and delivery than knowing that one is a participator and has an active role in the wondrous experience of giving birth.

Among the great fundamental biological rhythms, the progressive stages of childbirth, like the successive phases of sexual response, are governed by instinctive forces, but which at the same time reach the conscious level. At this point one may accept or reject them at will.

The woman feeling the contractions of labour or the woman experiencing sexual arousal is like a bather facing the surf for the first time. If he endeavours to stay upright, tense and unbending, he will be thrown over by a wave and will be frightened; if he relaxes and tries to follow its movement instead he will be able to land on his feet and he will be able to enjoy the sea. It may not be as easy for the modern woman as it was for the primitive woman to yield to these great natural rhythms, but it is certain that she will suffer if she resists. On the other hand there must certainly be a way of integrating into our contemporary world these phenomena in a positive fashion. If today's woman is too far removed from nature to follow spontaneously the waves, so to speak, then she must look with an open mind for ways to live these important events in a meaningful way.[43]

The significance of this ability to trust her body, "to ride with the waves" in labor and expulsion and trust those around her, is the precondition for experiencing childbirth as an ecstatic moment. Evidence from women who shared the experience of birth with their husbands and were fully conscious throughout the process indicates that the woman not only has a calmer and easier birth but remembers the experience as ecstatic.

Every woman who did report this on-rush of raptuous feeling . . . had her husband present. Without her husband at her side there was no rapture. . . . So it must be concluded that it is the husband's presence at delivery that is critical to a woman's linking of child-birth and ecstacy.[44]

The birth of my second child was a mixture of pain and great triumph. Having anticipated a short labor, Dan and I were at the hospital early. We worked hard during the day. I worked at my breathing exercises and he was helping me to keep my pattern of breathing regular. The pain was stronger than the previous time, though I kept control quite well. As time passed strong back labor began and I began to sense that the time was near. The nurses finally came to examine me and sent Dan out of the room. They discovered the membranes were not ruptured and so broke them. The first contraction after the water had gone felt like a kick from a horse. The pressure to push was intense so I began blowing off. "Dan! Get the nurse, the baby is coming!" No time (and no need) to call a doctor, no time to move me, so the British nurse took charge. With Dan holding my shoulders up I gave three or four big pushes and the baby was out. There in my bed, with the warm blood flowing gently on to the sheets, the baby was born. It was a glorious mess! Dan was not even robed in hospital garb. We had done it together. It was our event, ours and the two nurses. It was our triumph that we experienced in a cheerful little labor room in an atmosphere of warmth and informality. My only regret was that they did not bring the baby to my breast immediately, as they had done with the first one.

Trusting in the rhythms of her body, learning its pattern, and aiding its movement during both pregnancy and birth are not accomplishments a woman can achieve in loneliness and isolation. Physical and psychological preparation for the birth and the need for a trusting context for the event are essential, not only for a positive experience of birth, but also for the health of the baby and for the woman's adjustment during and after the birth.[45] Loneliness, isolation, and fear at a time of such personal importance lead not to an experience of ecstasy and fulfillment but to increased pain and distress at the powers threatening to overwhelm one. The crisis of birth for the woman involves her accepting her need of others and of being given that support.[46] Trusting in herself and her body depends upon having the love and support of others, particularly the father of the child. In that context the birth of the child may be experienced not only as a personal accomplishment of the woman but as the mutual achievement of two who find themselves standing breathless in front of the powers of nature acting through man and woman to bring forth new life. It is a power not our own, though we understand all its workings.

To be a part of that process, to see and participate in its workings, and to share in the active creative powers working in and through one's body is indeed a moment of joy, passion, ecstasy, mystery, and grace. The ability of female sexuality to give women the opportunity to experience that action of nature is a unique gift. We are thrown down by it, tremble at its force, and are humbled in front of it, for it speaks of the power of life to transcend us. In the birth of the child *we* are born again and we die. That new life symbolizes not only the end of a previous identity for the woman but also our own actual deaths. The new generation is born; we have participated in creating our replacements. Relaxing into birth and relaxing into death are not dissimilar. In each the physical process takes us with it. Women are fortunate in that through a personal body experience we can be taught the meaning of life and death, joy and fear, emptiness and fulfillment. In the context of a relationship of love and interdependence between man and woman, the experience of birth can not only deepen the woman's sense of herself but bind the relationship of mutual trust and sharing. In the absence of such a relationship with the father, the experience of birth may still be graceful if family and friends are supportive and one trusted individual can watch with the woman and aid the process of labor and delivery.

The possibility for a joyful experience of female sexuality in pregnancy and birth is open to women. Giving birth is a moment like no other—the experience of a mixture of pleasure and pain in an enormous passionate orgasmic effort. The ecstasy is *in* the experience and not only for the child that is born. The tragedy for many women is that the necessary ambiguity and fear never become transformed or integrated into a new self-understanding and acceptance of the goodness of the female body and its procreative possibilities. The bitterness and anger that remain can exercise destructive influence on the lives of other women as we teach one another the nature of the experience of pregnancy and birth and its role in the formation of a woman's identity. The attitude of the medical profession and men's fear of female sexuality have also contributed to women's inability to look to the experience of pregnancy and birth as of great value for their personal growth. The crisis of identity for the woman is spiritual. She must come to terms with a new self-concept, a view of her sexuality in its procreative role, and an understanding of its relation to her ongoing life and to the purpose of life itself. To find transformation through this crisis of pregnancy and birth would be for a woman to experience her body as fundamentally creative for her sense of identity as an individual and in her contribution to the lives of others.

8.

Parenthood

Becoming a mother is often experienced as the onset of post-partum depression! The triumphant act of giving birth and leaving the care of the hospital gives way to the woman's realization that she is now a "mother" and that this is supposed to be a glorious new role and feeling. Yet the great rush of maternal warmth that is supposed to flow toward this fragile little stranger suddenly catapulted into her life often fails to materialize. A woman's initial experience of the child she has intimately carried in her body for so many months is that it is alien to her. Its response to her individuality as its "mother" is minimal, and her own knowledge and power to care for it are limited by the lack of any previous relationship to this particular tiny creature and often to other small infants.

The act of having a child is the beginning of a fundamental identity crisis in the life of a woman. The depression she may feel in the first months after having given birth may indeed be partially determined by the total readjustment her hormonal system must make, but it is more significantly connected with her expectations and that of our society that the biological process of becoming a mother confers on a woman an immediate new sense of herself, a new feeling of her creative power as an individual, and a preeminent status in society. As a mother she anticipates being loved and respected; she looks forward to good feelings of warmth and security and the glow of deep satisfaction that nurturing and protecting the infant may bring. As a mother she will surely experience a new level of self-confidence in her powers and a deeper relationship with her husband. These expectations intensify the crisis of identity. She feels guilty for feeling strange in relation to the new child. She feels she should know how to be a "good" mother because she is the biological mother of the child. She is tested at the very core of her being to prove herself adequate in what is supposed to be the essential fulfillment of womanhood.

The emotions of the new mother are conflicting, both in relation to herself and to the child. The necessary ambiguity of becoming a mother is never mentioned in the myths about motherhood. Postpartum depression in this society may be more related to denying the ambivalent feelings than to hormonal changes. Denying the fears, the feelings of inadequacy, the strangeness, and the necessary hostility toward the baby can only deepen the crisis and drive the woman into increased isolation and ambivalence. To accept the fact that having a baby is by definition a critical event for both parents, but particularly for the mother, would open us to the possibility for gradual growth into a new identity and a recognition of the dangers along the way.

"Mothering is a process whereby the woman is always pulled between some ideal notion of what the 'good mother' should be and her own raw emotions."[1] At no point is Angela McBride's statement more true than in relation to the experience of nursing the baby. Women in large numbers are returning to breast-feeding these days, largely as a result of the efforts of the La Leche League. The physiological and emotional benefits of breast-feeding for mother and child are rightly stressed. However, in encouraging a practice that *is* inherently valuable, there is often a tendency to romanticize the image of the nursing mother and her sense of deep fulfillment that will emerge from the experience.[2] The "raw emotions" of the woman contain feelings of resentment and hostility as well as genuine physical pleasure and pride. Nursing a baby is inherently cannibalistic. A woman allows herself to be fed upon, to "be consumed." Erich Neumann describes nursing as a blood mystery: "After childbirth the woman's third blood mystery occurs: the transformation of blood into milk, which is the foundation for the primordial mysteries of food transformation."[3] Although the mother has fed and nourished the child through the long months of pregnancy, it was never a personal act. The fetus took from the mother's body what was available according to its own pattern. In nursing the relationship changes. To breast-feed is a personal act on the part of the mother. *She* feeds the baby; the baby grows. At every turn she feels personally responsible for the physical survival of the child. Her body fluid becomes its hold on life. There is a natural ambiguity to becoming part of the food chain in such an obvious manner for the sake of a small individual that cannot fend for itself. Ever leaving the child becomes fraught with fear: What if it cries and is hungry and I am gone, for I am its source of life!

Allowing oneself to be fed upon in such a manner does bring the woman emotional and physical rewards as suggested by the "guides to breast-feeding." As a natural body experience open to a woman, it can indeed be experienced gracefully. The physical sensation of being suckled is, once established, erotically pleasurable as an experience of female sexuality. The physical touching of naked breast to the baby's mouth and hands and the closeness of the body are warm and comforting, as indeed any intimate physical contact with another may be. Added to the known physiological benefits for mother and child,[4] are the emotional satisfactions that the woman derives from being able to see the child grow, fed by her own body. However, among the feelings of satisfaction are also resentment and anxiety. Being part of the food chain is *very tiring*; the child is literally *eating* you. Everything you eat or drink can become an occasion for anxiety, for every change in emotional state, every feeling of exhaustion can affect the milk supply. *You* as the nursing mother are not free to sleep through the night, to go away for the weekend. The child demands and you give, you give, you give.

The experience of breast-feeding, which is the initial experience of being a mother, symbolizes the more general ambivalence which is part of the new status of parenthood. Finding oneself and defining one's personal needs in face of what feels initially like an all-consuming monster is difficult. The total dependency of the baby on the mother and its absolute right to demand response, to cry out for attention, do not necessarily produce feelings of warmth and love; the mother may feel fragmentation, lack of self-determination, and hostility to that little crying mouth that sucks her dry. The ambiguity of the feelings of the nursing mother can be seen as the paradigm for the experience of parenthood; the biological role of nursing the baby, while an option and possibility only for the mother, is nevertheless a symbol of the tensions inherent within the role of parent. Having children is a commitment to a state of ambivalent emotions, wildly contradictory swings of pride, rage, and confusion as one struggles to meet each new stage of growth in a continually shifting focus of personal self-understanding.

The form of the new mother's identity crisis concerns finding a personal self-concept that includes her relationship to the child and does not destroy her sense of individuality. The spiritual dangers for the woman inherent in this identity crisis are particularly real in this society. A woman is forced to encounter herself at a radically new level; her old self dies, and a new self must be born. The physical act of giving birth happens quickly in comparison with the slow process of self-transformation during the years of parenthood. Nevertheless, the first months and years are the height of the storm and to a large extent determine what kind of self-image the woman will form and how it will affect her relationship to her children, her husband, and the life of future generations. In this struggle she must battle the demons, for the survival of her very soul is at stake. A woman's interpretation of her identity as "a mother" reflects her need to redefine the meaning of the process of life and her role within it. Her resolution of the spiritual crisis of identity will affect not only herself but the very lives of her children. The destructive possibilities for herself and her influence on others is never greater than at this point. On the other hand, at the heart of becoming a parent lies a potential for discovering growth and for realizing a more authentic form of human self-understanding as well as a clearer view of the nature and purpose of the whole of life.

The danger of having a child is that one will become a *Mother*. The biological role of mother in fact ends at the birth of the child or at least at weaning; from then on any other individual male or female can supply the child all its emotional and physical needs. Since we are human beings and not animals, the role that women play in relation to their children must be learned, even the ability to nurse. The biological role of a mother does not carry automatic behavior patterns into succeeding years. *Motherhood* is a learned role, controlled by social expectations and mythologies. To my mind, identifying with this mother image represents one of the most common and crucial false resolutions of the crisis. Moreover, the Mother is a concept of self-identity sanctified by religious institutions, the psychological profession, and social custom. For example, the ideal of the Mother as the "Eternal Woman" implicit within the Judeo-Christian tradition is described by Mary Daly:

> The characteristics of the Eternal Woman are opposed to those of a developing, authentic *person*, who will be unique, self-critical, self-creating, active and searching. By contrast to these authentic personal qualities, the Eternal Woman is said to have a vocation to surrender and hiddenness; hence the symbol of the veil. Self-less, she achieves not individual realization but merely generic fulfillment in motherhood, physical or spiritual (the wife is always a "mother to her husband" as well as to her children). She is said to be timeless and conservative by nature. She is shrouded in "mystery" because she is not recognized as a genuine human person.[5]

As this passage suggests, the role of the Mother is cosmic. She is an ideal, larger than life, and she senses herself and her role as that of a goddess.

The theory that becoming a Mother represents the fulfillment of a woman's instinctive, biologically given nature is also reinforced by psychologists. The biological basis of the Motherhood role is stressed by Haim Ginott:

To be mothered means to be nursed, diapered, cuddled, loved, played with, smiled at, talked to, and cared for: The need for maternal care is biologically determined. Lack of mothering endangers the infant's mental health and threatens his very survival. In contrast fathering involves less nature and more culture. Biologically speaking, father's contribution begins and ends before the child is born. All other fathering activities are socially determined.[6]

Dr. Ginott's view that *mothering* is a biologically determined function and *fathering* is a learned cultural role represents an understanding of the nature of the role of motherhood common to our society. *Mothering* means perfect love and nurturance.[7] The quality of love that a mother gives is seen as quite different in kind from all others. Erich Fromm, for example, describes mother-love as "unconditional," whereas father-love is "contingent."[8] In this image a Mother always gives, without question, without reservation. She cannot help but care for, nurture, and love. "The motivation for this (caring) behaviour, experienced as mother love, is the pleasure which the female derives from the fulfillment of her instinctual nature."[9]

A woman who attempts to find her new identity in this mythic ideal will find it destructive for herself, her child, and her husband; it will foreclose forever the genuine spiritual possibilities of personal growth in relation to children. Women who identify with the mythology of Motherhood attempt to live out an ideal in which total loving, giving, and responsibility for the happiness of all are a woman's deepest creative expression. This myth is not only a projection of the male ideal of the all-caring mother[10] but also unfortunately represents a common view that women have of the new identity being offered to them by the act of giving birth. The type of mothering that their mothers gave them as children and the quality of the relationship established between their mother and father become the instinctive basis for the new identity unless a woman can reflect on her internalized expectations.

Mothering as a role involves conceiving oneself as essentially responsible for the emotional and physical growth of the child and for the emotional life of the family unit. A woman as mother is supposed to be more in tune with the emotional needs of the child and husband; she is supposed to be more sensitive and more responsive and therefore can supposedly anticipate and fulfill the needs of others. Elizabeth Janeway suggests that this image reflects an assumption that women were first taught to feel by their mothers.[11]

The restrictive aspect of internalizing the motherhood myth is that it causes a woman to be unable to relate to her genuine and rightful destructive feelings.

The burden of being responsible for everyone's happiness is enormous and produces an army of frustrated, unhappy mothers. And the myth is perpetuated that happiness is bestowed in childhood by a placid mother-fairy rather than developed through a lifetime of hard work in coming to terms with your own problems and possibilities.[12]

To internalize this myth that one's identity is essentially more self-giving and other-directed than that of any male leads a woman ultimately to mother her husband as well as her children. In this behavior lurks not only destruction of the self but destruction of respect for the integrity of the other. The woman learns to play a fundamentally dishonest role that deceives the self as well as the other. Angela McBride's quotation of Dr. Joyce Brothers's description of the role the young mother should now play toward her husband reflects the destructiveness of attempting to live out the Motherhood mystique:

It all adds up to offering your husband only your best self. Forego the luxury of indulging in moods of irritability, discontent, and envy. These are luxuries. It means one more strike against you in your effort to keep the irreplaceable treasure—your husband's romantic love. . . . Your problem is to be sure you remain a woman, just as alluring, feminine and interesting to your husband as before the advent of the child. That, in addition to your responsibility as a mother, will give you a very, very fulltime job.[13]

The deceptive element of the Motherhood myth is that it represents a false understanding of personal power and pride. Mothering results in an idealized notion of one's personal control over the child and the nature and quality of one's influence upon it. Internalizing the prevailing Motherhood myth tempts a woman to see herself as the essential giver of life, the one who not only protects and nurtures but also controls the formation of the child's identity. In giving "mother love" to a child, a woman often pours out her own unfulfilled desires on the child and completely smothers him or her.[14] Too much that is given the name *maternal love* reflects the needs of the woman as she seeks to find meaning for herself through the child. Manipulative "mother love" is never given freely but expects a response, a coo, a smile, a touch, and later on a gift, a Mother's Day card. The one who gives all for the sake of her children may believe in her virtue as the "giver of all," but in reality she demands repayment in the form of affection, dependence, and worship by her husband as well as her children. To internalize the image of the great Mother Goddess in her perfection can blind a woman to her individual needs and to the limits of her power. It is a demonic resolution because she cannot recognize her destructive effects on others.

The mythology of the primitive religious cults recognized clearly that she who is the giver of all life also devours and destroys life. Erich Neumann's discussion of the image of the goddess in his book *The Great Mother* documents the fact that the positive image of the goddess as she who brings forth life and sustains is balanced by a view that the Great Mother is also responsible for death. The Terrible Mother is the other side of the Great Mother. She is appeased by sacrifices of blood and death.[15] These primitive rituals reflect an understanding that life and death are essentially bound together, and yet their import for the contemporary woman is clear. The source of all life is also experienced by the child as dark and destructive. If a woman attempts to define her new identity essentially by being loving, giving, and self-sacrificial, she will in fact destroy the very life she is trying to foster, as well as her own self-respect and sense of worth. She will ask the child to live for her, to provide the reason for her happiness, to be her essential fulfillment as a woman. No adult, let alone a small child, can carry that burden and develop his or her own sense of independence.

The possibility for an enriching experience of having children lies in a woman not becoming a Mother. In the emotional search for self, acknowledging rather than sublimating real feelings, fears, and guilt is essential for transition into a new form of self-understanding. It involves recognizing that the journey into new identity will be painful and anxious, feelings not peculiar to a woman as a biological female but part of the very ambiguity of the parental role. Sharing those feelings and entering the despair of nonexistence that the early months of parenthood may bring is the route to new growth in the self. Guilt because a woman does not fulfill the expected Motherhood role can intensify the despair and frustration.

The social framework of our pattern of family life also increases a woman's feelings of isolation and total responsibility. Unless a new pattern of social behavior can emerge, a woman will feel inherently responsible for rearing the children. However, no person should be in that much control of a child's development. A woman for her own sake and for the sake of the children must conquer the mythology which causes her deep guilt when she separates herself from the child and pursues her own activities. The inability to separate herself, to define and pursue her own goals during the child-rearing years, represents an ultimate lack of trust in herself and a misconception of the graceful potential inherent in being a parent.

A woman and a man become parents at the birth of the child. The baby is a stranger to both. It is the beginning of a relationship between the child and both of its parents. The tragedy of our view of the essential "motherliness" of women is that we exclude men from any essential relationship to their offspring. We have assumed from the beginning that "mothers know best," and so indeed soon they do since they learn from experience. The possibility for a mature resolution of the crisis of identity for the woman at the arrival of a new child into her life

is that her new role and that of her husband consist of learning
how to become a parent and not how to become a mother.[16]
The possibility for giving up the traditional self-image of the
Mother lies also in the father giving up the traditional role of
Fathering and in also allowing others to become "parents" of
the child. In our social structure men have excluded themselves
and have been excluded by women from the potential that being
in contact with children can bring to their own growth as individuals. Women have assumed that the traditional role of raising children is both their fate and their right. Neither traditional
role can lead to the experience of parenting as transforming;
indeed *parenting* must transcend the sexual stereotypes of
Mothering and Fathering.

A child in itself is a "gift." It is a stranger hurled into life and
into the presence of two stuttering individuals. A child is never
"my child" as the possession of the mother or the father. The
"otherness" of the baby is an essential part of the initial experiences of being a parent, and in face of that otherness we are
shaken and amazed and often reserved. As humans we need
time to get to know one another, and so it is with a child, even a
small baby. It has its own autonomy, and we must respect it.
The supposed immediate flow of maternal warmth that fills
women reflects the myth of Motherhood. Many women (and
men) sense no immediate warmth and identity with the child.[17]
I believe the potential for gradual growth into new identity as a
parent indeed depends upon this initial recognition of the
unique separateness of the baby. As a tiny "other," the child is
not hers, his, or theirs. They do not possess it. The suddenness
of the child's appearance, whether born or adopted, can remind
us that we are in a sense "foster" parents whose responsibility
and opportunity is to allow the child to grow according to its
own structure and inherent possibilities. It is a gift of life; we
did not make it, nor will we make it grow. These initial feelings
of reverence and respect for the wonder of the individual life-
process entrusted to our care can, I believe, provide the paradigm for understanding the new identity of being a parent open
to the woman and to the man.

Recognizing the essential separateness of the child can provide the basis for the woman being able to find a sense of her identity which includes her role as a parent but is not identical with it. A woman must retain her "virginity," her sense of unique purpose in life, which cannot be lived out by her children. Her sense of self-worth must continue to be "in herself" and cannot depend upon the response of the child to her. In that sense then, a woman must sacrifice her children; she must separate herself from them, both to give them room to grow and to rediscover her autonomy as a woman. Esther Harding in her book *Women's Mysteries* described this process of giving up the maternal role as the "sacrifice of the son."[18] In many ancient religious mythologies the mother goddess allows her son to die. Harding suggests that these myths represent an important psychological necessity for women that requires an act of courage. To find identification in her child seems so natural and is sustained by the Motherhood myth:

Externally it looks so admirable for a woman to sink her interests in those of her child, and to sacrifice her own comfort and well-being at every point in order to further his interests. It is only later that the true nature of her course of action shows itself. Then, when the son's complete inability to face the hard realities of life, his total absence of self-discipline and his incapacity to take a responsible attitude, bear dolorous witness to the falseness of his upbringing, it is usually too late to remedy the situation.[19]

"Sacrificing the son" or giving up the Motherhood role is an ordeal. A woman may feel guilty and fearful that she is not doing everything for her children. Nevertheless, overidentification with this self-image represents a fundamental lack of trust in the necessary growth into individuality on the part of the child and in her own necessary growth process of self-discovery:

The woman's impulse to protect and cherish another, to keep him a child and save him from the hardness of life, to mother him in short, is closely related to the self-protecting impulse which prevents her from facing life's reality and the intensity of her own emotions, for herself.[20]

By relinquishing her position of superiority as giver, facing her emotional needs, and giving up her dependency on her children and the role of Mother, a woman opens up the possibility for sharing the experience of parenthood and for rediscovering her finiteness as human.

I had a big battle with my daughter tonight. She was overtired (probably had no rest at day care today), overexcited and perhaps had a tummy ache from too many Easter eggs. (Yes, I know that was my fault too, I should have put the Easter basket up as soon as we came home. God knows how many she ate at school!) She didn't want to go to bed. I think she was feeling pretty badly about my leaving the room to put Nicholas to sleep when Dan was gone too. She wanted to fix the seats on the bicycles. Maybe it was my fault but she seemed in such a "contrary" mood that I thought it best to get on with the process of bath and bed. There was no way to "jolly" her along—the tantrum started before we even got upstairs. I proceeded with the "continue what you are doing with calm but firm intent" sort of behavior but it didn't work. How do you get a screaming, kicking child undressed when she doesn't want to?

I was getting mad by this time, Stephanie hotter and more furious and coughing more. Oh God. How do I get out of this one? (a) Calm her down, (b) Proceed towards bed. Thinking that it is undignified to struggle with a child, I took her into her room, put her in bed and shut the door and went away to let her scream it out. The rage continued; and she began banging on the door. After a decent interval I thought I would offer an olive branch, a cup of juice. She spurned the juice, took off downstairs and crawled into her "crying chair." After awhile I joined her, took her on my knee and calmed her by stroking her hair. She was so hot and tired. We watched the hockey on T.V.

After she had cooled down somewhat, I began talking about reading stories and going upstairs again. I carried her upstairs and as we got to the bedroom the tantrum started all over again. By this time I had skipped the idea of a bath. I managed to get her dress off. I was struggling with my child. By this time my sense of frustration was alarmingly high. She kicked and twisted like crazy as I tried to put on her diaper, I was aware that my potential for violence was increasing sharply, having smacked her bottom to get her to stop struggling (how foolish of me of course, it enraged her further). I put my arms around her tightly and said very angrily and loudly how mad I was with her and that she was going to get her pajamas put on. It didn't help a bit.

At that point my own fear about how I was acting and the realization of how impossible it was to dress her in this situation made me give the pajamas to my totally nude daughter and say you put them on. Then I turned off the light and firmly shut the door. Regretting the decision to leave her in the darkness, I went back in. Something seemed to have changed. I put her top on with a little resistance, after that she dived in bed and lay there—exhausted probably—and I put on the rest. I wiped her hot face with a damp cloth and then she got up and put her arms out. I turned off the light and held her in my arms, singing lullabye songs, twinkle, twinkle and rockabye baby. She was so tired. She lay limp in my arms while I rocked her. I put her in bed, kissed her, stroked her damp hair and said goodnight.

Never before have I experienced that transition so quickly from rage and hate, being the ogre, the stern mother, to the tender, comforting loving, warm mother. No wonder she hates and loves me. I hate and love her. I am terrified of the power she has to unleash emotions in me, my loving and my raging. I don't think of myself as a violent person, but I know through her that I am. I am horrified at what I can unleash in her—the tantrums, such rage! I live every day with the guilt, the ambiguity, the sense of uncertainty about each of my actions. I want, like every other parent in the world, to be a good parent, and never before has anything conspired to make me feel more inadequate, more anxious and guilty, more insecure. Our poor children. You have the power to destroy all falsity and reduce us to see us as we are, humble us to see ourselves with all our superficial masks torn away! The sight is painful.

Parenting provides women and men with a unique opportunity to understand themselves and form a new perspective on
the meaning of life. In relating to children every aspect of oneself becomes manifest; every emotion in love, tenderness, hatred,
and despair becomes revealed. In responding to the life of a
child the possibility for growth in self-knowledge is presented to
a man and to a woman as in no other relationship. Every aspect
of one's personality becomes known; feelings of failure, guilt,
insecurity, ambivalence, and anxiety often predominate. In
admitting feelings lies the hope for growth in self-understanding.
The vulnerability of the child causes us to see our own vulnerability as human beings. We do not *know* what is best; at no
time can we be sure that we are doing the right thing. The
ambiguity of the role of Mother described by Elizabeth Janeway
as particularly related to her personal responsibility for raising
children in a time of transition in this society and with no social
supports[21] is, in my mind, not only connected with the particular cultural situation of women, but with the nature of parenthood itself. The future is always unknown. Becoming a parent
means opening the doors to the radical ambiguity of life.

As parents we are "failures" before we ever begin. We know
that our children will hate us, curse us, and accuse us in the future, as we do our parents. In spite of all the reading, advice, and
proper preparation, this knowledge of failure may sometimes
make us despair. And yet, the recognition of failure brings the
realization of grace. We as parents are human. We may make
every effort to "do the right thing," but we are not finally in
control. This tension between being responsible and yet knowing that we cannot see the outcome of all our actions is the
sobering reality of parenthood. The moments when a child has
an accident or narrowly escapes injury are times of preparation
for the real tragedies of parenthood when our children die.
These moments of escape often turn into recrimination, accusa-
tion, and guilt; our hearts stand still, we die a thousand deaths.
But these moments can be occasions of grace if we can go
beyond the sense of failure. They can reveal to us that we are
not gods and goddesses, perfect parents able to control and

foresee every eventuality. Our limited power and understanding comes to face us. Growing in this moment involves not only "learning one's lesson" but trusting in the process of life. We as parents are inevitably inadequate. We are human. We make mistakes; we are negligent. We take risks. However, the process of life is itself a risk, and we can learn through parenting how to trust its capacity to reveal good and to bring evil.

"Letting go control" as a parent involves trusting this process of life, knowing and accepting that many times we will fail and create evil and not good in our children. Life also continues in us and through us; our children move beyond us. In wishing to do the best for our children, we manifest our hopes for the future. To hope *is* realistic; we have a unique opportunity to influence the future by raising children. Nevertheless, the moments of grace come not only in the fulfillment of our hopes but in the depths of our despair. Trusting, accepting, and expressing all our emotions is the means not only for growth in self-awareness but for the enrichment of our understanding that the process of life transcends us, moves beyond us.

Raising children puts us close to the awareness that the very structure of life moves toward the future, and in this action we as parents participate and witness but never control. Parents are "watchers" of their children. As each stage of growth occurs, we may be reminded that like gardeners we are part of an inherently mysterious process. We may know the factors that influence growth, we may try to provide the best emotional and physical conditions for the growth, but we do not make growth. The richness of parenthood lies in being able to observe this natural process. It can remind us of the ongoingness of life and its power both to amaze and to horrify us. As each child grows according to his or her own unique genetic and environmental mixture, we can be reminded of the power of life to create individuality and the unique potential of each living creature.

Children therefore represent a distinct opportunity for psychological and spiritual growth for women and for men. Seeing ourselves "in miniature," we can learn to reexperience every childlike emotion in ourselves; the total physicality of small infants and young children brings us back in contact with our bodily feelings, our simplicity, and our desire for warmth and touch. The immediacy of children's emotions, their laughs and tears and their fantasies and anxieties, are gateways to our own positive "childlike" selves and "childish" feelings. *Our* childishness as adults, our wish to be protected and dependent, comes forcibly into view as we find ourselves becoming angry at our children's insecurity. If we can recognize, in the expectations and hopes that we have for our children, that we are speaking of our own unfulfilled desires, we will prevent ourselves from manipulating our children. The temptation of parenthood is to expect our children to be what we never could be, to do what we never could do. In recognizing that the natural hopes we have for our children reflect our own unlived dreams, we may come to recognize our fears and unfulfilled potential and live it out ourselves, rather than expecting our children to embody all we could not be.[22]

As in every other identity crisis, the test of becoming a parent for the woman involves a death and rebirth of the self. The potential for a demonic resolution of the crisis is particularly powerful for the woman in this society. Lacking a sense of her own worth, she may look to the Motherhood role and to the children to supply her with a reason for existence and a total focus for her identity as a woman. The demonic effect of this is that her love for the children will be coercive and doomed to failure for "the most traditional women, whose sense of worth comes only from others, can never be loved enough."[23] Raising children can offer women and men, on the other hand, an occasion for growth that involves moments of renewal. In coming to terms with our own strengths and weaknesses and our ambitions and fears for our children, we can learn over a period of years to see ourselves more honestly and more completely and break through the false notions of identity and the cultural myths that have shaped our being. We can learn to redefine the meaning of self-acceptance and trust in ourselves, and in so doing we can give our children what they need most, our trust in them and in the process of life.[24] With this trust we will be able to respond to each change, each new crisis, in the life of the child. The crisis of identity involved in parenthood is not undergone once, but continually. Embarking on that action involves women and men in testing their own identities, perhaps more radically than any other experience. Being true to one's deepest needs (though perhaps not to one's immediate desires) in the act of parenting is a constant challenge, and yet this is most likely to serve the needs of the children.[25]

Women *need* children in the same manner that men need children, not to be their ultimate fulfillment but to be the possibility for revealing the nature of the mystery of life in its wonders and tragedies. Living in relation to children may be self-revealing as we see ourselves for what we are, accept that knowledge, and find hope in the very ongoingness of life both in ourselves and in our children. It is in process of the "formation" of the other that I am myself formed anew; in that experience of being formed I may often feel torn asunder; old aspects of my self-conception must die in order for my new transformation into selfhood to take place. As a parent I may experience that necessary re-formation of myself in humility, sorrow, and joy.

9.

The Change of Life

Mary Wollstonecraft, writing at the end of the eighteenth century, cited an "unnamed gentleman" who wondered what possible use a woman over the age of forty had on this earth.[1] This unkind speculation reflects a real problem: What possible use do I have in my later years? My youthful beauty is gone, my childbearing years are over, and my fertility disappeared with the advent of menopause. The physiological hormonal alterations of the "change of life" often coincide for the unmarried and the married alike with an identity crisis common to the middle years in men and women.[2] The physiological changes of menopause come at a time when the structure of life shifts—children grow up and move away, husbands reevaluate their masculine identity, often searching for affirmations of their worth through changes in career or through sexual escapades. The divorce rate in our society peaks for men and women in their middle years, struggling to find a new identity for the remainder of their lives.

This midlife crisis is preeminently, however, a woman's crisis. A woman's fertility *definitely ends*, whereas a man's gradually tapers off. The hormonal changes that accompany menopause *may* cause varying degrees of unpleasant physiological symptoms—the renowned hot flashes, irregular bleeding, mood changes. Medical journals refer to this phenomenon as "degeneration" of the female body structure.[3] There are changes in skin elasticity; there are changes in the bones and in the vertebrae which can eventually lead to "dowager's" hump and loss of height. Women fear the possibility of breast cancer and hysterectomies. The menopausal period is also a time of psychological danger, for female suicides are at one of their peak levels (the other is in early adulthood, 24–34 years).[4]

In our modern times it is claimed that the use of estrogen therapy can prove helpful to many women in alleviating the so-called degenerative processes and mitigating some of the unpleasant physical symptoms associated with hormonal changes. Is this all there is to it? Are we to assume with the makers of estrogen that better hormone therapy will successfully handle "the change of life"?

Today, this upheaval in a woman's body can be avoided. The intelligent woman will not unnecessarily accept undue and rapid aging. Her physician will be able to determine when she is on the threshold of her "change of life." And it is within his power to alleviate these symptoms so that the continuance of life becomes more vital, healthier, and happier.

[In response to the issue of depression the pamphlet advises] "menstrual blues? cheer up. Gather up all those 'somedays'—someday you'll do this, someday you'll try all those wonderful things and start making them come true!"[5]

I believe that this approach to menopause, which is now being questioned as to its long-term effects, does *not* sufficiently recognize the nature of this crisis to enable a woman to come to a new form of self-understanding.

The change of life is a crisis for the married and the unmarried woman that is as significant as the onset of menstruation. It marks the end of one life and the beginning of another. Menopause is not, however, as sudden as the onset of menstruation. Over a three- or four-year period the inevitable process occurs, and one day the menses is gone. Fertility is over.

Primitive women rarely faced this last crisis of sexuality. As actuarial tables show,[6] the average life span of women has lengthened dramatically over the last one hundred years. Better medical care in childbirth, the advent of birth control, and limiting the size of families means that most women do have a life—a whole other third of their lives—*beyond* the childbearing years. In earlier times a woman did not survive beyond her fertility. There was no real role for them outside of childbearing; thus Jesus was particularly concerned about the plight of widows. In light of these circumstances, primitive societies have no "rites of passage" for the woman's loss of her fertility. Women beyond childbearing age were not even regarded as women; they were seen as men.[7] There is no folk wisdom or religious rite to interpret this most significant change in a woman's life. It is a change that *needs* symbolic interpretation, for it, above all others, presents itself initially as a death, an end, a decay, a degeneration.

The need of the modern woman to find a symbolic framework for this fundamental stage of life is acute. She needs a new basis for self-understanding outside her earlier interpretation of her sexuality. The issue facing her is whether she can find new purpose, new identity, new worth, a new self-concept, and a new sense of ultimate meaning as she passes into middle age. The crisis is more than a physiological adjustment to declining hormone levels. A woman must come to terms with herself and the meaning of life on a radical level. Perhaps the reason this crisis is so difficult and has so many aspects is that it foreshadows the end, death itself, the last crisis. The end of a woman's fertile years intimates the decline of the whole body and signifies a gradual approach toward the end of its powers in death. Menopause unmistakably marks the slowing of the whole system before we are ready for it. In midlife we are still strong; we are often healthy, and yet one element of our body's creative powers is now over and forces us to recognize our gradual movement toward death.

For this reason the crisis of menopause affects married and unmarried alike. For the never-married it can represent the loss of an unrealized potentiality—childbearing. The end of my fertility may bring regrets, for my freedom of choice concerning the use of my female procreative powers is now over. Even if I have gladly forsaken bearing children for other values in earlier years, whatever regrets there may have been are now intensified, and I may question the rightness of past decisions. What would it have been like to bear a child? I face impending old age aware that I will have no one to care for me.

For the never-married or the once-married menopause may also signal the end of hopes for being able to find a life partner. Marriage without the possibility for childbearing, while greeted with joy in the later years, may appear an unlikely possibility for a woman facing menopause. She fears that the end of her fertility is the end of her sexual attractiveness. She fears that the hoped-for union which has eluded her or failed her in earlier years is now finally beyond her grasp. She is alone forever and will never experience her bodily capacities as a mother or find her sexuality fulfilled.

For the married woman who was never able to conceive, menopause represents the end of a dream. Being unable to conceive is a deep sadness for many women. Wanting to conceive and being unable to do so leads to real regret even though children may have been adopted. The process of being able to conceive, of giving birth, is significant, not only because of the child, but because it can symbolize a woman's strength, a valuable element of her psychosomatic personal unity. For her, as for others at menopause, lingering hopes and regrets surface and must be dealt with.

For the married woman who enjoyed her sexuality as the bearer of children, menopause may also be full of regrets. There will never be any more children; her biological role of mother is now over. Menopause is a particularly deep crisis for women who have devoted themselves exclusively to mothering. The children are often grown up and leaving home as the woman wonders who she is now that her role as mother seems to be over. The demands of parenthood are over; the house is quiet, and the woman asks herself, Is there anything left? The end of her role of mother carries no accolades, no promotion, no thanks. The children are often grateful to be gone after the confrontations of the adolescent years. The woman who has found her identity exclusively in mothering faces the crisis of middle life with the least resources. She may find her physiological symptoms part of a larger crisis in which the essential elements of her very life are uprooted. She feels tricked and cheated and that her children are ungrateful. She experiences, not joy that the demands of parenthood are over, but *emptiness*. The promise given to her that she will find herself through motherhood has proven hollow. She is no longer "needed," no longer loved; she feels no productive role in society.

The mythology that suggests that motherhood is the essential role of the woman is most cruel at this point. The years that are filled with doing for others, often to the exclusion of self-interest and self-development, of striving to fulfill the ideal of the good mother, end, not with a sense of fulfillment, but in confusion, and with a lack of preparedness and inner resources to cope with the changes.[8] The paradox of a woman's attempt to live up to the traditional image of the mother or wife who gives her life for her children is that she above all has neglected her personal and spiritual development. For such women, the change of life brings the hardest challenge.

The change of life is indeed *a change* and offers a woman the possibility for a new direction and focus for interpreting her identity in relation to the meaning of life as a whole. If she feels that her life is over now that her sexual attractiveness begins to decline, she will also feel an ever-increasing sense of insecurity about her worth as an individual. Our culture emphasizes youthful female sexual attractiveness as the major criterion of female worth and thereby engenders fear and mistrust in the middle-aged woman. Compulsively reaching for cosmetics, fad diets, and youthful clothes can be a way of dealing with this anxiety. This sort of resolution is only temporary. More energy and time will continually be spent on packaging the exterior to fit the youthful self-image and hiding an ever-deepening inner sense of insecurity.

Another manner of handling the crisis of middle age, more

familiar to men than to women yet common to women perhaps more in fantasy than in reality, is to have an affair. To find oneself as a woman again, to solve the crisis in sexual identity by searching for sexual fulfillment in a new love, may indeed feel like a resolution of the crisis. The rejuvenation brought about by feeling loved, not in the firm body of a young woman but in the body of a mature woman bearing the stretch marks of motherhood, can bring new feelings of self-worth. To be loved in *this body* by one who finds you attractive as you *are* and not in the memory of what you *were* can bring new self-confidence and joy. This resolution, however, does not in fact prove lasting or finally satisfactory for negotiating a new form of self-understanding. Looking to others, whether lovers, substitute children, or a new husband, only as a means to escape the confusion of personal identity will lead to increasing bitterness and demands upon those to whom we reach out. The potential for falling into this form of demonic resolution of this major crisis is strong in our society that emphasizes youthful sexual attractiveness and/or motherhood as the exclusive definitions for female identity.

Our society also places great value on achievement. The woman, like her male counterpart, who has attempted to find herself in a career, generally faces a severe midlife crisis. She realizes that she is no longer a "promising young hopeful." She feels undermined by younger women and sees the future as gradually more closed rather than infinitely open. Her creative powers seem to have settled into boredom and frustration.

How then can the contemporary woman find grace rather than destruction in the change of life? To come through the crisis with a new focus on oneself, a new sense of one's female identity, is important, not just for the woman herself, but in terms of her attitude toward others and her effect upon all her significant others. Possessiveness, lack of trust in others, feelings of insecurity, frustration, and blame can characterize the woman from the middle of her life onward. Her friends and family attempt to withdraw from the emotional burdens she places upon them.

To discover new depths of self-understanding requires first of all a recognition of the nature of the crisis. The physiological symptoms of menopause and any affects that they have on mood may be helped by chemical means. The problem is that the woman finds it difficult to distinguish what part of the depression is caused by changes in her life situation and what part is a result of hormonal imbalance. Separating the physiological from the psychological factors is indeed impossible. As in all other life-crises there *is* a distinct physiological process at work. In some women it has marked effects; in others, almost none. In fact, women who have felt very well during pregnancy may be "estrogen sensitive"[9] and experience more depression postpartum and during menopause. To recognize the nature of the crisis in both its physiological and its emotional forms is essential for a graceful resolution. Hormonal therapy, if proved safe, may indeed ease the physical changes, but the personal issues need to be recognized in all their implications for a new life-pattern.

Something dies at menopause; the fertile female potential is over. For this there needs to be mourning as well as thankfulness. The ability to experience a new body, free from menses, free from the fears of unwanted pregnancy, depends, I believe, on acknowledging and grieving for what is no longer—the end of one stage of life. All the joys and sorrows, hopes and disappointments, connected with the experience of one's sexuality in its procreative function need expression. Acknowledging this sorrow and expressing it without guilt to oneself and to others will eventually enable new hope to emerge. The new self cannot grow until the process of mourning and grief has been completed.

There is new life and new identity beyond the change of life. This crisis, perhaps more crucial than the others since it extends over a period of years, calls us to an awareness that the process of dying may be slow and will encompass the regrets, the guilt, and the painful coming to terms with that which remained unborn, both physically and spiritually. The change of life is a reordering of the personality and of the body. For there to be a new order, the old one must be displaced. As we go through the change of life, we do not know that the new order *will* emerge. We only know that the familiar forms are slowly eroding; the body chemistry is changing. The pattern of life is changing, and the values of the old life are being challenged. This feels like death, and we have no hope that there can be anything new.

The crisis of menopause may indeed involve physiological changes. It is, however, essentially a spiritual crisis. During the change of life I am challenged to come to terms with what I have left behind, with whatever I have done or not done with my female sexuality in its procreative aspect, with whatever I have done or not done in my youth with my early vitality. Midlife is a time for mourning; it is also a time to forgive oneself and others. It is a time for reassessing one's worth as a woman, as a unique individual; it is a time for realigning and rediscovering one's ultimate value in relation to the whole.

The ability to recognize the nature of this crisis, to express the fears, confusion, regrets, and bitterness, will allow the individual woman to come into a new life as the process of mourning for the end of youth gives way to the reemergence of hope. Life comes, for out of the end of the old, something new emerges—perhaps unbidden. Risking, trusting the future, finding hope that new forms of personal self-understanding and worth will emerge are qualities that are given, *discovered*. The new identity, the new strength, the new direction that can emerge for a woman as life changes come not so much from conscious planning but from parts of the self hidden and unexpressed for many years.

The outcome of the change of life can be truly graceful if one avoids desperately hanging on to an old identity and a fixation with a single view of one's female sexuality. The new body may indeed, once achieved, offer a new hope, a new freedom of female sexual expression. Released from the anxiety and fear of pregnancy forever, many women achieve a new freedom, a deeper level of sexual expression and vitality. Sexuality returns to its autonomous nature in its nonprocreative aspect, and a woman can enjoy it in a new way. Freed from menses and her particular pattern of psychosomatic responses to the fluctuation in hormone levels, a postmenopausal woman is offered a new body relieved of any possible discomfort associated with menstruation. Her physical health may be better, and her spirit may be better as the burdens of her procreative sexual being are left behind.

Middle life represents a crisis. The old breaks up so that the new may emerge. The woman must decide whether she will trust the open future or attempt to hold on to the past. Many will break the old patterns of relationships and risk the insecurity of the future, the loneliness, and the self-doubt. Divorce, separation, and new ventures in education and careers are all characteristic of this stage. Risking the future always includes leaving, loneliness, and spiritual reckoning in which the self struggles with the agony of self-doubt. Enrichment will emerge if the risk is made; new strengths will be found, new forms of self-understanding will emerge, and new relationships will be formed.

The change of life offers a woman the possibility of coming to terms with her unique individuality outside of (though inclusive of) the procreative nature of her sexuality. She is now free to come to terms with herself. She need no longer sacrifice herself for the sake of her children or the achievement of her husband. She can give attention to her own values and worth, her own sense of creative center, and her own responsibility to the life that is within her. Freed from obligation, false achievements, making it financially, and living for others, a woman may discover that the change of life offers her the possibility of discovering herself in a new manner.[10]

Perhaps the mythological image of the Virgin Goddess is an appropriate symbol for this stage of a woman's spiritual journey. The Virgin Goddess has risked and suffered, born children, and loved many. She is a virgin, however, because she finds her sense of spiritual wholeness within herself; she is a woman unto herself. The movement of life that propels us ever forward toward death is nevertheless not identical with physical decline but can be seen as a spiritual journey reaching to deeper levels, as the Jungian psychologists have suggested.[11] The change of life offers a woman a new opportunity to recognize her buried strengths, to realize the wholeness of her identity. New directions, new forms of creativity, new levels of self-understanding can emerge, and a woman finds freedom to *be* herself.

The change of life opens the door for a blossoming of the spirit. It may be a time for more inner activity. The preceding years busy with external activity in the "productive" phase of life, both physically and mentally, can now give way to a time of inner productivity—a psychological and spiritual growth of the total woman.[12] Irene Claremont de Castillejo writes "if we are wise we shall notice that our concerns change too. As we advance in years the inner demands which have rightfully lain dormant during youth, claim our attention more and more."[13]

The question that must be answered by the individual is, Who am I now that my life begins its descent toward death? What am I worth now that my primary productivity is over? What does my female identity mean as I leave my youthful sexuality behind? The need to find an answer to these questions is acute; the manner in which the crisis of the change of life is handled will determine how the woman experiences herself in the gradual process of aging. If she emerges from the crisis with a new sense of self-trust, with a new belief in her creative role in the universe and in relation to others, and with a new sense of joy about the potential strength in her own maturity as a woman, she will be able to face the final crisis of life, the anticipation of death. Indeed these years postmenopause bring many trials for the woman. In our culture, given the extra longevity of women, it is most likely that she will eventually face burying her husband. During these years illness may impinge on her life; aged parents may need to be nursed and buried. These are the years when the woman will of necessity be more involved with death and the intimation of death. Where will she find strength to face the separations involved—the loss of children from the home, the loss of parents by death, the possibility of widowhood or of reaching the awareness that one will have to negotiate the post-retirement years alone? The ability to discover the strength lies in trusting oneself as an inherently worthy individual woman, letting go of the past, and embracing the future. The trust that there are always new levels of growth for the woman even as the past patterns recede and our relationships are forced to change through separation and death is an ability to trust in the movement of life itself. That is why the crisis of the change of life is spiritual.

Many women are freed by the change of life from past limiting patterns of interpretation of sexual identity. Broken marriages often result. Emerging from the crisis of the change of life enhanced and not diminished is a blessing, not merely for the woman, but for those around her. The destructive solution to the crisis may mean bitterness, regrets over the past, blaming husbands and children, a false sexual self-image in desperately striving for youth, displacing the mothering image on others in manipulation and control, feeling insecure and worthless, losing hope. Without hope there can be no life, no value, no joy.

Irene Claremont de Castillejo describes the individual psyche as a garden that we are responsible for tending to enable it to grow. It is a spiritual responsibility, not only to ourselves, but also for others.

It is in the latter part of life that people need to turn attention inwards. They need to do so because if their garden is as it should be they can die content, feeling that they have fulfilled their task of becoming the person they were born to be. But it is also an obligation to society. What a man or woman is within affects all those around. The old who are frustrated and resentful because they have omitted to become in life the persons they should have been, cause all in their vicinity to suffer.[14]

The crisis of the change of life can therefore be a process of death and rebirth, a change from the old life into the new. There will be some suffering, and yet from that it is possible for the woman to build a new sense of female identity. The tragedy of this crisis is that the possibility for grace may never come, and many women find themselves facing the process of aging with ever-deepening despair and dread. The discovery of the hidden creative powers within is unfortunately never made, and the woman fails to enrich the lives of those she touches. To find new trust is, however, to be reborn through the change of life and is an experience of joy for the woman and those around her.

10.

Anticipating Death

Old. *Old!* That word frightens me. Old woman. *You* are an old woman. You are an *old* woman. It sounds like a curse, an insult, a condemnation. It carries the feeling of silliness, stupidity, senility. I don't want to be old. To be old is to be dead, to be nothing, of no value to myself or anyone else. Old woman! I fear it. I fear admitting that I too am old. How can I accept that I am old because nothing we value in this society is old?

As a woman the last and most significant crisis for my spiritual identity is coming to terms with the meaning of my "declining" years. This last stage of life is indeed built upon the previous stages, and my ability to find grace in the so-called golden years depends on the ability I found to have a creative sense of my personal identity in and through the many previous stages of life.[1] The stage of old age in woman and man brings many hardships and fears of a practical nature. Retirement, the death of a spouse, sickness and physical infirmity, forced dependency on others, loss of sight and hearing, financial insecurity, changes of residence, lack of mobility, loneliness, and the fear of death are all possible hardships. And yet people do grow old differently; they do die differently. Some old women decline into despair, self-pity, and bitterness; their world shrinks around them as their perspective on themselves and their lives closes in. For such women old age is a living death; their spirits have died already, and there is no hope, no belief in themselves or in their ultimate significance to life to sustain them. Their days of usefulness to society are over, and they can find no value in the present day or in the years ahead. They look only backward to a self and a life that is now gone.

There are, on the other hand, those burning bright spirits whose old age is a period of splendor. These are the wise old women at whose feet the younger generation will gladly sit. They enrich their own lives and the lives of those they touch. Their love of life, of themselves, of the new, and of everything around brings grace to all. What is it that makes the difference? How may I find enrichment in my old age and fulfillment in my later years even in the face of many hardships? How can I accept my old age and anticipate my death without fear and terror and live my last period of life joyfully, within whatever limitations I may find? How can I avoid senility, despair, and a living death? These are the crucial questions facing a woman as she moves into old age.

Aging is a crisis for men and women; retirement is a crisis for men and for women, and yet the particular manner in which a woman experiences this crisis depends largely on her self-understanding and on her interpretation of herself as a woman in her social roles. The advent of old age in this culture is particularly hard on women because of the stress on a youthful self-image. To be young is good; to be old is bad. There is, as gerontologists have pointed out, a form of discrimination in modern society, particularly the North American, which is as pervasive as racism and sexism. They have termed it ageism.[2] To be old is to be nothing, not fully a human being. Once the "productive" years are over, you are finished. The crisis of identity caused by this cultural framework is evident when people reach retirement. When we are old, we are considered useless to society; our physical and mental capacities are seen as weak or outdated. We may no longer exercise power or responsibility, and the younger generation begins to treat us as children. When we are old, we are presumed irresponsible, in need of protection from ourselves. We live to please the younger generation, not ourselves; we are powerless in a world dedicated to the worship of youth.

As a woman I must deal with the general negative cultural framework concerning old age, and I must also deal with being an old woman. What does it mean to be an old woman? How can I love myself in my own old age? How can I love my face, my body? How can I love my gray hair, my wrinkled skin, my old hands? The alternative is to hate myself, to despair, to find my aging body disgusting, and to attempt with all my power to disguise that fact with cosmetics, dyes, and youthful clothes. The crisis of old age for a woman is particularly concerned with body image. Women should be young and beautiful; men want sexy women. What is a woman when she is no longer young or beautiful? Is she an old hag? How can I find a self-image which accepts my aging face and body and finds beauty in them?

Women in this culture must shut their ears and eyes to the media and the projected images of women. To find beauty as an old woman is not to find it in attempting to recapture the colors and shapes of youth. The old woman painted and rouged with wigs and bangles is a tragic figure, a travesty of female identity. For her, each passing day, each new wrinkle or pain, is the sign of a losing battle in the need to stave off the advance of age, the intimations of death. For her, old age can only be a frightening experience, an everlasting quest to appear young. This solution to the advent of old age is self-deceptive, for it finally robs the woman of any chance to bring new levels of meaning to her self-identity. She struggles to survive in the competition with younger women. She spends all her energy and money on keeping up appearances, and the *real* work of old age, the important and necessary psychological and personal tasks, remain unfinished, and life is incomplete.

In order to come to a new self-image in old age a woman needs to defy the culture around her; too much exposure to youthful images of woman can indeed drive her to despair and anxiety. Studies have shown that too much exposure to television's "Pepsi generation" can increase senility and our sense of hopelessness.[3] Shutting our eyes to the visual images of woman found on television and in advertising, turning our backs on the cultural view of the old woman, is not only a possibility but a *necessity* if we are to grow emotionally, psychologically, and spiritually and be able to discover a sense of purpose and peace in our old age.

How then can I be an old woman creatively? How may I accept my aging body and find a new sense of myself that will sustain me into my death? Pretending desperately to be young is one particular limiting solution to the crisis; another tempting form is also socially acceptable—being a "grandmother." If I look to old age as my opportunity now to be only a grandmother, I will give up a sense that my own life has any more growing to do. In living for the younger generation I will push them to please me, to give me attention. My value to myself will be found only in terms of their loving me. I will look to them to give me a purpose for living. I will spend my time bragging about my grandchildren, attempting to influence the way they are raised, and complaining when my advice is not followed. Grandchildren are beautiful joys, but living one's life for them, dependent on their response, can become manipulative and controlling and be resented by the younger generation. In this culture children often live far away, and any continuing role in relation to the younger generation cannot presume the proximity of families. If there are children in one's life, they will prove a blessing, as indeed they do for anyone, but the role of grandmother will be insufficient for a new self-understanding of oneself as a woman in old age. Writing of the narrowness and pettiness of many old people, the members of a group called the Phoenix Club advocate the need for older people to detach themselves from exclusive concern with the activities of children and grandchildren.[4] As old women or old men we have our own lives that are essentially productive in their own manner. Too much concern to be a grandparent can rob us of that sense of our purposes in life.

Old age can only be experienced as graceful if it is recognized as a crisis. The psychologist Erik Erikson characterizes the crisis by two terms, *integrity* or *despair*.[5] By this he means that the spiritual crisis, the crisis of coming to terms with aging and one's approaching death, can lead either to a new sense of wholeness, self-trust, and trust in the universe, or it can lead to the loss of hope and an attitude of regret and bitterness. There is a choice to be made about how to interpret the meaning of one's old age and death. If the last ten or twenty years of one's life have no meaning to oneself, to others, or ultimately to the whole, then indeed one may sink into despair.

The crises of old age and of facing death are most clearly spiritual, for they involve finding a framework, a value system, a sense of personal worth in one's womanhood that transcends even one's life. The spiritual and psychological "business" of old age is to come to terms with that value. The crisis of old age is not undergone in a day; it is a lengthy process of bringing the self together, of fitting the pieces of the past into a whole. The different women that one has been, the young girl, the lover, the mature woman, are all collected and accepted as parts of the total self.

There is an important task in old age for reviewing, for re-assimilating, for storytelling, and for coming to terms with previous disappointments and failures.[6] We need to forgive ourselves; we need to learn to have no regrets about what we did and did not do. We need to free ourselves from the burden of guilt about the past. Married or unmarried, widowed, divorced, with children or without, that process is now finished, and our need in old age is to find ways to let it be finished. The business of old age is therefore not to pretend to be young, or to live for the young, but to live at last and most completely for ourselves and pay attention to our inner needs. The self, that creative center of energy, is there ready to express itself. Old age can and should be a time for creative and artistic self-expression, in words, poetry, and intellectual creativity.

Irene de Castillejo advocates that every woman should find a way to tell her life story, perhaps by writing an autobiography or a novel. Finding people to listen to our stories may be difficult, but finding ways to express ourselves can be of unique worth for ourselves and for future generations.[7] If we listen to ourselves, we can indeed find ways to express what is most truly our inner selves. Though physical strength may decline, the life of the mind and the artistic spirit can flower in a manner most true to the self.[8]

For many women who have never had the opportunity for intellectual growth, old age provides the first time to delight in learning and study. For others, retirement years provide the opportunity for growth in new skills, the expression of unfulfilled parts of the personality. A woman can look to old age as a time to discover the parts of herself that have remained hidden, and she can at last speak for herself and herself alone. Husband and children can be companions in this endeavor, but she must wean herself finally from identifying her life with theirs. This is perhaps the most critical task for the woman, particularly in this culture where women who have been raised to be dependent on men are outliving their men.[9] A woman can quite fairly expect to be a widow if she has married.

Does it sound cold-blooded to look at you, my husband, and anticipate that I shall probably have to bury you and live on without you? What will happen to me in those last years? Will living alone again be full of fear? Will I know who I am once you are dead? How shall I prepare myself for those days? Will I cling to you desperately as you die because of my fear of life without you?

Old age is a special crisis for women because so many of them must deal with becoming widows. Widows have to live in a more exclusive female society in old age. The chances for remarrying are small, especially since men tend to marry younger women. Old age will involve, therefore, for most women living alone, living without the man around whom one may have defined one's life. Old age will mean having to find new comfort and strength in the company of other women. Old age may mean having to find a new sense of myself as a woman not in relation to a man.

Old age may also mean a new crisis for my sexuality. Perceived by the world as a neuter, I am still warm, tender, capable of passion, longing for touch, and the caress of my body. Will old age and widowhood mean sinking into sexual oblivion and living in frustration and anger?[10] Old age may mean risking myself physically in relationships that are not socially approved —outside of marriage, with younger men, expressing myself through touch in all my friendships. Old age may mean having to find this new sense of myself as an individual and a new joy to life even though my husband is dead. I can so easily find myself sinking into despair, loneliness, self-pity, and memories for the past. How can I overcome the desperation, the fear, and the sense of loneliness to discover something new in myself that can live? As in any death, the hope for new growth and life can come only through immersion in the process of grieving and mourning and being allowed to accept and express sorrow. Accepting the need for grieving for what is gone will enable us to discover new life and friendships even in the seeming collapse of a whole way of life and the sense of who we are.[11]

Living alone, being placed more extensively in the company of other women, can be a destructive experience if our only understanding of being a woman is based on a relationship to a man. Learning to like other women can be a new experience for the widow. Older women competing desperately with one another for the few available men is a sad sight. It is sadder still for women to feel they must live out their later years according to the criteria of the earlier years. Old age can bring its own distinctive fulfillments; it can be a time of new friendships with other women, of companionship, of support and kindness. Finding these qualities of love and friendship will prove finally more graceful than hastily contracted marriages reached for to stave off the fear of loneliness.

Learning to live alone in old age is indeed a necessary prerequisite for facing death. By living alone I don't necessarily mean living physically alone, but living alone spiritually, at one with oneself, paying attention to one's own needs, thoughts, and desires. Much of this living alone may be in terms of memories, expressing and reliving them mentally. Women, who frequently have lived so much of their lives in relation to others and have defined themselves by others, may need to discover the renewal present in their own aloneness, in their own unique history, personality, and qualities. Separating oneself psychically from husband, children, grandchildren, from all unnecessary tasks and obligations is the sacred responsibility of old age. Indeed, the ability to endure the crisis of widowhood and to approach your *own* death depends upon having an already acknowledged sense of your separate identity as a woman. For some women widowhood liberates the self; the creative journey in self-discovery and self-trust begins when a constricting interpretation of the role of oneself as a wife is finally left behind.

Dealing creatively with old age for women and men involves coming to terms with the fear of death. If our fear of death can be expressed and recognized and death can be acknowledged not as a remote possibility but as an fairly imminent reality, we may indeed be able to overcome the terror of old age and experience each day as a blessing, a gift. Making concrete provisions for death, disposing of our property and beloved possessions, can give us a sense of peace. Old age can indeed be a time of freedom from fear of death, from the need to live in anything more than the fullness of the present moment. The pretenses of the past can be stripped away; it is time to be oneself, without apology, without self-deception. There is nothing to be lost and everything to be gained by reaching out, risking to be our real selves. In those encounters we will find meaning and a new sense of self-acceptance. Life will be filled with joy.

Those who are able to find strength in old age have a perspective on their own death. Facing death means essentially acknowledging one's anxieties about it. Facing death also means coming to some form of understanding about the meaning of my life as an individual woman which ultimately transcends my death. Carl Jung writes of the pervasiveness of the doctrine of immortality in all the world's religions. Having a sense of trust that our lives have an ultimate significance through death appears necessary to a transforming experience of old age. Jung suggests that we can live more comfortably in a house if we do not fear that the roof will imminently collapse.[12] Finding a sense of one's ultimate worth that will survive death is perhaps the most important task of the stage of anticipating death. This might express itself in traditional religious terms in a belief in the survival of the soul, or it may find expression in a sense of accepting our contribution to the ongoing process of life, however small that may be. Reaching a sense of an ultimate worth for my life as an individual woman is necessary to enable me to experience my old age gracefully and to accept my coming death. However many days there are can then be lived fully to the end.

Reaching this sense of ultimate worth has indeed been spoken of as essential for graceful transition through all the previous life-crises. A sense of ultimate self-acceptance, self-love, is only possible if my self-image as a woman is not based on any particular age, role, relationship, or view of myself. Knowing that I am enriched and deepened by the many changes of my life, that I am continually growing even to the last day, will be the basis for discovering grace in old age and in face of death. Elizabeth Kubler-Ross's book *Death: The Final Stage of Growth*[13] also stresses the point that even in the process of dying we may experience life as graceful if we open ourselves to others and express our fears and feelings. In that communication we will discover love and strength as all false self-images and pretenses can finally be released.

Negotiating the last stage of life is the same as finding grace in the earlier stages. It involves the same acknowledgment of the negative elements of experience. There is a need to vocalize the real anxieties that necessarily accompany aging and dying. Old age is a drag. Dying is a bore. Finding grace in old age does not lie in trying to be the sweet old lady, gentle and undemanding to the last, resisting help out of some misguided notion of "coping perfectly well." Being able to accept our dependency may be particularly hard for the woman who has always been healthy, has always sacrificed herself for other people, and has spent her life serving others. That role too we will have to let go, and we will have to accept that we are at a time in life when we need other people to help us and eventually to nurse us. Knowing that we are of value to ourselves and to others, not just in terms of what we do physically for others, will enable us to come to a new understanding of what we can be for other people, most essentially ourselves.

Old age is a time to transcend the narrow interests of family activities and the filling of days with an endless round of trivial "entertainment" to make the time pass more quickly. Old age is a time for serious thought, for immersion in the ongoing process of life in all its forms that enables us to wonder at our very existence. Women who have been cheated of an opportunity to develop themselves in the intellect or the artistic spirit find themselves most severely handicapped in old age.[14] Having lived their lives exclusively in relation to husband and children, they are unable to find happiness in old age when these roles are left behind. Satisfaction in old age depends on discovering this unique sense of self and expressing it to others. The loss of husband, the absence of children, the death of old friends can indeed then be borne without a descent into despair because I know that my identity as a woman is not solely limited to my relationships with family or friends. I am myself; I must express that to the world. My life-long task is to discover how to reveal the myriad aspects of my own self to myself and to others. This sense of self-trust is the meaning of the word *grace*. Feeling that I am accepted by others, by myself, and by the whole movement of life in which I find myself as a woman is indeed a gift. I *find* it. It is given to me. Even in the moments of dying to the old self that characterized the transition through the many stages, I discover something new emerging. In the final stage also I find it—a sense of completion, a sense of my ultimate value as a human being, a sense of the worth of my life and my woman-hood.

There is a choice, however, that is made either explicitly or implicitly. Grace only comes by risking. This is the sense of what Tillich means by "the courage to be."[15] To experience old age and death as a stage of growth involves risking onself, breaking through, letting go, trusting in oneself and in all the gamut of emotions and insights that are one's own. If we cannot be honest in old age, when can we be honest with ourselves?

Knowing ourselves is most crucial now if we are to find peace and a sense of completion. Women who have been taught that they are to live for others often ignore this personal spiritual task and will spend their last years complaining and bitter about all that they suffer and all that they have missed. The effect of this is truly demonic, for it drives the old woman into despair, and her effect on others is destructive and causes resentment. Cruelty, resentment, guilt, rigidity, selfishness, and petulance are the effects of failing to risk oneself in relation to others. Such old people are a blight on all they meet. Becoming old does not automatically convey wisdom and grace. The old hag *is* a real possibility, destructive of life and hope in herself and in others. False self-images, false pride, pretensions, and illusions may indeed cause depression, anger, despair, and isolation in old age. Only if we have the ability to recognize the crisis for what it is, struggle with the need to let go of our now outdated goals and perspectives, can we find a new sense of our uniqueness as women—not identical with youth and beauty, not identical with our various roles as career woman, grandmother, or wife. This disassociation must be undergone for the new sense of our unique worth and continuing purpose to emerge. By finding our own sense of self-fulfillment we will indeed enrich the lives of others and find excitement and wonder and love in every passing day.

We do grow old and die differently. It is our responsibility to to others as well as to ourselves to risk ourselves; our lives *can* be creative to the last, or they can be painfully destructive. This is true most clearly at the end of our lives when despair in the face of aging and death appears such an inevitability. Transcending despair and finding renewal even in the company of increasing limitation and suffering depend on risking our selves. This is what religious people mean by faith—the experience of feeling ultimately accepted, whether by what we call God or the ongoing process of creative life. As women this act of faith or trust implies overcoming the negative self-image, the tendency to self-distrust and despair that is part of a cultural framework for old women.

I hope I can age gracefully, tending to my body with the dignity it deserves, cultivating the things that express my spirit with new enthusiasm, and communicating all that I am becoming in what I do. In this perspective, becoming complete in understanding my identity as woman will never be finished. There will always be new thoughts, new feelings to experience, new friendships to discover. I can live with the sense of the unfinished nature of my life, for it is not a feeling of incompleteness but rather an awareness that my goal in life is to *live* as long as I have breath. Living is loving, flowing out of ourselves toward the whole universe. Only by being truly ourselves, by loving ourselves as women, can we be graceful in our effect on others.

The image of the woman at-one-in-herself, the ancient Virgin Goddess who loved many and lived richly, is needed in our act of dying. Dying is the highest act of individuation possible, the ultimate act of freedom, courage, and faith.[16] As women we can face suffering and death if we believe in our uniqueness and in our ultimate value to life itself.

Epilogue

Becoming woman is not a process that is ever finished except, perhaps for oneself at any rate, in the moment of death. The task of finding oneself is never completed, but each stage of life brings its own possibilities for renewal and joy and sorrow. There is no fixed female identity. One element of a false solution to life is to stagnate in one identity, one stage, one self-image of womanhood. Each of us is many women, and each stage of life offers the potential for discovering new freedom, new growth, and new pleasures. There is also a necessary sloughing off of the old woman like layers of skin so that we can become the new woman. The life of a woman is like the life of every living creature; it is a series of transitions involving death and rebirth. In human beings, emotional and spiritual development is, however, not inevitable. We do *choose*; we are free to effect what we become even at the last moment of our life. Sometimes we despair that nothing can be done; we have been determined by our childhood, our society, our culture, our age, and there is no hope. We women often tend to see ourselves determined by forces and structures outside of ourselves, our biology, our personal and social condition, and our self-interpretation. Though change may be much harder the older we become and the suffering we will endure to undergo change will intensify, a woman's life is her own; she *is* free to live gracefully or demonically right to the last.

154

Becoming woman is a spiritual quest of believing in one's unique self, one's freedom to find the transformation in each stage of life. If a woman can trust life, she will find that the action of existence brings renewal; out of despair, hope, and wonder, and love will emerge. The psychological and spiritual dangers are real, however; becoming woman involves risking. "Hell on earth" will result from relying on false self-images of womanhood. The demonic potential of these choices in their destructive effect on ourselves and others is evident wherever frustrated and unhappy women meet the lives of others.

Becoming woman is a spiritual search. It involves finding a sense of one's personal worth in relation to the whole of life, even beyond death. Believing in ourselves, loving ourselves as women, is our most sacred task in and through the many phases of our sexual and personal development. Finding freedom from fear involves risking and trusting our feelings. As we risk, however, we will be given new hope, new strength, and a new love for ourselves and for others. Acting on this trust will enable us to grow in understanding through all the stages of life.

Notes

Introduction

1. Erik Erikson, *Childhood and Society*, 2d ed. (New York: W. W. Norton, 1963). Erikson's theory of the psychosocial stages of development was first proposed in this book and explicated further in his studies on adolescence and the identity crisis.
2. Richard Rubenstein, *After Auschwitz* (Indianapolis: Bobbs Merrill, 1966).

Chapter 1

1. Simone de Beauvoir, *The Second Sex*, trans. and ed. H. M. Parshley (New York: Alfred A. Knopf, 1952), p. 295.
2. *The Miracle of You* (Toronto: The Life Cycle Centre, Kimberly-Clark of Canada, Ltd.).
3. Ibid.
4. Judith M. Bardwick, *Psychology of Women: A Study of Bio-Cultural Conflicts* (New York: Harper and Row, 1971), p. 48.
5. Karen E. Paige, "Women Learn to Sing the Menstrual Blues," *Psychology Today*, September 1973, p. 46.
6. Germaine Greer, *The Female Eunuch* (St. Albans: Granada Publishing Ltd., 1971), p. 89.
7. See W. Gifford-Jones, *On Being a Woman: The Modern Woman's Guide to Gynecology* (Toronto: McClelland and Stewart, 1969), pp. 28–31, 34.
8. Erich Neumann, *The Great Mother*, trans. Ralph Manheim (Princeton: Princeton University Press, 1963), p. 31.
9. Paige, "Women Learn to Sing the Menstrual Blues," p. 43.

10. Margaret Mead, *Male and Female: A Study of the Sexes in a Changing World* (New York: Dell Publishing Co., 1949), pp. 183–86.

11. Maria Leach, ed., *Funk and Wagnall's Standard Dictionary of Folklore Mythology and Legend*, vol. 2 (New York: Funk and Wagnall's, 1950), p. 707.

12. James Frazer, *The Golden Bough*, vol. 1, abridged version (New York: Macmillan Co., 1942), p. 600.

13. Mead, *Male and Female*, pp. 178–211.

14. James Frazer, *The Golden Bough*, 3d ed., vol. 3, part 2 (London: MacMillan and Co., 1922), p. 250.

15. Joseph Campbell, *The Hero with a Thousand Faces* (Princeton: Princeton University Press, 1949), p. 154.

16. M. Esther Harding, *Women's Mysteries: Ancient and Modern* (New York: G. P. Putnam's Sons, 1971), p. 90.

17. Neumann, *Great Mother*, p. 290.

18. Harding, *Women's Mysteries*, p. 87. See also Viola Klein, *The Feminine Character: History of an Ideology* (Urbana: University of Illinois Press, 1946), p. 96.

19. Joseph Campbell, *The Masks of God: Primitive Mythology* (New York: Viking Press, 1959), p. 370.

Chapter 2

1. Erik Erikson, *Young Man Luther: A Study in Psychoanalysis and History* (New York: W. W. Norton and Co., 1958), p. 14.

2. Mircea Eliade, *Rites and Symbols of Initiation: The Mysteries of Birth and Rebirth*, trans. Willard R. Trask (New York: Harper and Row, 1958), pp. 3–9. See Erich Neumann, *The Great Mother* (Princeton: Princeton University Press, 1963), p. 175.

3. See, for example, Joseph Campbell, *The Hero with a Thousand Faces* (Princeton: Princeton University Press, 1949), and Hermann Hesse, *Narcissus and Goldmund*.

4. Elizabeth Gould Davis, *The First Sex* (Baltimore: Penguin Books, 1972), p. 38.

5. Eliade, *Rites and Symbols*, pp. xiii–xiv.

6. Mircea Eliade, *The Sacred and the Profane: The Nature of Religion*, trans. Willard R. Trask (New York: Harcourt, Brace and World, 1959), pp. 192–95).

7. Eliade, *Rites and Symbols*, p. 47.

8. J. S. La Fontaine, ed., *The Interpretation of Ritual* (London: Travistock Publications Ltd., 1972), p. 178.

9. Eliade, *Rites and Symbols*, p. 41.

10. Mircea Eliade, *Myths, Dreams, and Mysteries*, trans. Philip Mairet (London: Harvill Press, 1960), pp. 217–18. See also Bruno Bettelheim,

Symbolic Wounds: Puberty Rites and the Envious Male (New York: Collier Books, 1962), p. 136.

11. Erik Erikson, "Inner and Outer Space: Reflections on Womanhood," *Daedelus*, vol. 3, 1965, as quoted in Phyllis Chesler, *Women and Madness* (Garden City: Doubleday and Co., 1972), pp. 76 ff.

12. Bruno Bettelheim, "The Commitment Required of a Woman Entering a Scientific Profession in Present Day American Society," *Women and the Scientific Professions*, MIT Symposium on American Women in Science and Engineering, Cambridge, Mass., 1965, as quoted in Chesler, *Women and Madness*, p. 77.

13. See M. Esther Harding, *Women's Mysteries: Ancient and Modern* (New York: G. P. Putnam's Sons, 1971), p. 246.

14. Caroline G. Heilbrun, *Towards Androgyny: Aspects of Male and Female in Literature* (New York: Harper and Row, 1973), p. 91.

15. Erik H. Erikson, *Identity: Youth and Crisis* (New York: W. W. Norton and Co., 1968), p. 96. Erikson uses the term *regression* in the service of the ego as an aspect of the ego's creative use and return to earlier stages.

Chapter 3

1. Mircea Eliade, *Australian Religions* (Ithaca: Cornell University Press, 1973), pp. 116–18.

2. Audrey I. Richards, *Chisungu: A Girl's Initiation Ceremony among the Bemba of Northern Rhodesia* (London: Faber and Faber, 1956), p. 33.

3. Elizabeth Gould Davis, *The First Sex* (Baltimore: Penguin Books, 1972), p. 160.

4. Ibid., pp. 160 ff.

5. Erich Neumann, *Amor and Psyche: The Psychic Development of the Feminine*, trans. Ralph Manheim (Princeton: Princeton University Press, 1956), p. 63.

6. Ibid., pp. 63 ff.

7. B. Z. Goldberg, *Sex in Religion* (New York: Liveright, 1930), pp. 64–65.

8. Simone de Beauvoir, *The Second Sex*, trans. and ed. H. M. Parshley (New York: Alfred A. Knopf, 1952), p. 384.

9. Ibid., p. 348.

10. Ibid., p. 391.

11. See Donald W. Hastings, *Sexual Expression in Marriage* (New York: Bantam Books, 1967), p. 37. "Tradition has it that females come to sexual arousal more slowly than males. However, this well-entrenched concept has been challenged by Kinsey *et al.* (1953) who feels that it is based on a misinterpretation of the facts. Using as the criterion the time involved to reach orgasm via masturbation, he found that 'the female is

not appreciably slower than the male to reach orgasm.' However, if the time to reach orgasm via coitus is the criterion, the female does respond more slowly than the male."

12. Irene Claremont de Castillejo, *Knowing Woman: A Feminine Psychology* (New York: Harper and Row, 1973), p. 94.

13. Ibid., p. 96.

14. Rollo May, *Love and Will* (New York: W. W. Norton and Co., 1969), p. 54.

15. M. Esther Harding, *Women's Mysteries: Ancient and Modern* (New York: G. P. Putnam's Sons, 1971), p. 147.

16. Ibid., p. 162.

17. Sydney Janet Kaplan, "The Limits of Consciousness in the Novels of Doris Lessing," *Doris Lessing: Critical Studies*, ed. Annis Pratt and L. S. Demt (Madison: University of Wisconsin Press, 1974), p. 129.

18. Ibid., p. 132.

Chapter 4

1. Erik Erikson, *Identity: Youth and Crisis* (New York: W. W. Norton and Co., 1968), pp. 135 ff.

2. Ibid., p. 137.

3. Denis de Rougement, *Love in the Western World*, trans. Montgomery Belgion (New York: Fawcett Publications, 1956).

4. Erich Fromm, *The Art of Loving* (New York: Bantam Books, 1963), pp. 17 ff., 84.

5. Patricia O'Brien, *The Woman Alone* (New York: Quandrangle/New York Times Book Co., 1973), p. 43.

6. Percival M. Symonds, "Differences in Attitudes towards Love and Sex," *Marriage and the Family in the Modern World*, ed. Ruth Schonle Cavan (New York: Thomas Y. Crowell Co., 1969), p. 138.

7. Judith M. Bardwick, *Psychology of Women: A Study of Bio-Cultural Conflicts* (New York: Harper and Row, 1971), p. 149.

8. Erich Neumann, *Amor and Psyche*, trans. Ralph Manheim (Princeton: Princeton University Press, 1956), p. 110.

9. Robert M. Stein, *Incest and Human Love: The Betrayal of the Soul in Psychotherapy* (Baltimore: Penguin Books, 1974), p. 93; cf. p. 94.

10. Ibid., p. 95.

11. Erikson, *Identity: Youth and Crisis*, pp. 261–94.

12. Ibid., p. 283.

13. Ibid., p. 273.

14. Bardwick, *Psychology of Women*, p. 151.

15. Martina Horner, "The motive to avoid success and changing aspirations of college women," *Readings on the Psychology of Women*, ed. Judith M. Bardwick (New York: Harper and Row, 1972), pp. 62–67.

16. Luther is quoted by Irving Singer in *The Nature of Love from Plato to Luther* (New York: Random House, 1966), p. 366.

17. Ibid.

18. Edward Edinger, *Ego and Archetype* (New York: G. P. Putnam's Sons, 1972), p. 161.

19. Fromm, *Art of Loving*, pp. 48–53.

20. Pope Paul VI, *La Documentation Catholique*, no. 1482, col. 1923, 1966, quoted by George H. Tavard, *Woman in Christian Tradition* (Notre Dame: University of Notre Dame Press, 1973), p. 137, italics mine.

21. Fromm, *Art of Loving*, p. 19.

22. Snell and Gail J. Putney, *Normal Neurosis: The Adjusted American* (New York: Harper and Row, 1964), p. 127.

23. Fromm, *Art of Loving*, pp. 20–22.

24. *Meister Eckhart*, trans. R. B. Blakney (New York: Harper and Brothers, 1941), p. 204, cited by Fromm, *Art of Loving*, p. 53.

25. David G. Jones, "Love and Life Goals," *Love Today*, ed. Herbert A. Otto (New York: Dell Publishing Co., 1972), p. 228.

26. Abraham Maslow, *Toward a Psychology of Being* (New York: Van Nostrand Reinhold Co., 1968), pp. 137 ff.

27. Fromm, *Art of Loving*, pp. 103–4. He speaks of faith as an essential ingredient in love of self and of others.

28. Irene Claremont de Castillejo, *Knowing Woman: A Feminine Psychology* (New York: Harper and Row, 1973), p. 124.

29. Ibid., p. 125.

30. Ibid., pp. 129–30.

31. Henry Winthrop, "Love and Companionship," *Love Today*, p. 108.

Chapter 5

1. Mary Ellmann, "The Bell Jar: An American Girlhood," *The Art of Sylvia Plath*, ed. Charles Newman (Bloomington: Indiana University Press, 1970), p. 226.

2. William J. Goode, *Women in Divorce* (New York: Free Press, 1956), p. 191.

3. H. Z. Lopata, *Widowhood in an American City* (Cambridge: Schenkman Publishing Co., 1973), p. 45.

4. Robert Neale, *The Art of Dying* (New York: Harper and Row, 1973), pp. 49–70.

5. Patricia O'Brien, *The Woman Alone* (New York: Quadrangle/New York Times Book Co., 1973), p. 41.

6. Howard B. Lyman, *Single Again* (New York: David McKay Co., 1971), p. 247.

7. Martina S. Horner, "Feminity and Successful Achievement: A Basic

Inconsistency," *Feminine Personality and Conflict,* ed. Judith Bardwick et al. (Belmont: Wadsworth Publishing Co., 1970), p. 55.

8. O'Brien, *Woman Alone,* p. 33.

9. Mel Krantzler, *Creative Divorce: A New Opportunity for Personal Growth* (Scarborough: New American Library of Canada, 1975), p. 86.

10. Ibid., p. 57. See also Russell Becker, *When Marriage Ends* (Philadelphia: Fortress Press, 1971), p. 19.

11. Lopata, *Widowhood,* p. 55.

12. Krantzler, *Creative Divorce,* p. 70.

13. Neale, *Art of Dying,* p. 69.

14. James Hillmann, *Suicide and the Soul* (New York: Harper and Row, 1964), pp. 88–89.

15. Isabelle Taves, *Women Alone* (New York: Funk and Wagnall's, 1968), pp. 41–60.

16. Ibid., p. 50.

17. Goode, *Women in Divorce,* p. 212.

18. Ibid., p. 216.

19. Lopata, *Widowhood,* p. 88.

20. Peter Marris, *Widows and Their Families* (London: Routledge and Kegan Paul, 1958), p. 56.

21. Krantzler, *Creative Divorce,* pp. 113, 146.

22. Ibid., pp. 166, 168. Brackets mine.

23. Carl Gustav Jung, *Collected Works,* vol. 6, rev. R. F. C. Hull, trans. H. G. Baynes (London: Routledge and Kegan Paul, 1971), para. 787.

24. Edward Edinger, *Ego and Archetype* (New York: G. P. Putnam's Sons, 1972), pp. 160 ff.

25. Ibid., p. 178.

26. Erik Erikson, *Identity: Youth and Crisis* (New York: W. W. Norton and Co., 1968), pp. 91–135.

27. Jung, *Collected Works,* vol. 14, para. 13 ff.

28. Ibid., para. 14, n. 69.

29. Edinger, *Ego and Archetype,* p. 163.

Chapter 6

Jessie Bernard, *The Future of Marriage* (New York: Bantam Books, 1973), suggests there is evidence for saying that marriage is more psychologically destructive for women than for men (pp. 30 ff.).

2. Gibson Winter, *Love and Conflict: New Patterns in Family Life* (Garden City: Doubleday and Co., 1958), pp. 26 ff.

3. Ibid., pp. 51 ff.

4. M. Esther Harding, *Women's Mysteries: Ancient and Modern* (New York: G. P. Putnam's Sons, 1971), p. 121.

5. William J. Fielding, *Strange Customs of Courtship and Marriage* (New York: Garden City Publishing Co., 1942), p. 19.

6. Judith M. Bardwick, *Psychology of Women: A Study of Bio-Cultural Conflicts* (New York: Harper and Row, 1971), p. 210.

7. M. Esther Harding, *The Way of All Women* (New York: G. P. Putnam's Sons, 1970), p. 121.

8. Winter, *Love and Conflict*, p. 23.

9. Simone de Beauvoir, *The Second Sex*, trans. and ed. H. M. Parshley (New York: Alfred A. Knopf, 1952), p. 431.

10. Margaret Mead, *Male and Female: A Study of the Sexes in a Changing World* (New York: Dell Publishing Co., 1949), p. 313.

11. Bardwick, *Psychology of Women*, p. 210.

12. Ibid., p. 211.

13. Dudley J. Chapman, *The Femine Mind and Body: The Psychosexual and Psychosomatic Reactions of Women* (London: Vision Press Ltd., 1967), p. 197.

14. Bernard, *Future of Marriage*, p. 345, table 27. (Table 27 originated from a HEW document, *National Center for Health Statistics, Selected, Symptoms of Psychological Distress*. U.S. Department of Health, Education and Welfare, 1970. Table 17, pp. 30–31).

15. Kathrin Perutz, *The Marriage Fallacy* (London: Hodder and Stoughton, 1972), p. 37.

16. Bernard, *Future of Marriage*, pp. 43, 48.

17. Alice Rossi, "Transition to Parenthood," *Journal of Marriage and the Family*, February 1968, as quoted in Bernard, *Future of Marriage*, p. 43.

18. Karen Horney, *Feminine Psychology*, ed. Harold Kelman (New York: W. W. Norton, 1967), p. 124.

19. Chapman, *Feminine Mind and Body*, p. 182. See also Harding, *Way of All Women*, p. 60.

20. Elizabeth Janeway, *Man's World, Woman's Place* (New York: William Morrow and Co., 1971), p. 205.

21. Bernard, *Future of Marriage*, p. 321.

22. See Harding, *Women's Mysteries*, pp. 110 ff.

23. Ibid., p. 147.

24. I originally developed this concept of the importance of "virginity" for women in "Differentiation and Difference—Reflection on the Ethical Implications of Women's Liberation," *Women and Religion*, rev. ed., ed. Judith Plaskow and Joan Arnold Romero (Missoula: American Academy of Religion and The Scholar's Press, 1974), pp. 127–37.

25. Deane William Ferm, *Responsible Sexuality Now* (New York: Seabury Press, 1971), p. 119.

26. Nena and George O'Neill, *Open Marriage: A New Life Style for Couples* (New York: Avon Books, 1972), p. 160.

27. Ibid., pp. 52–53.

28. Ibid., p. 188.

29. Ibid., p. 50.

30. Mircea Eliade, *The Two and the One*, trans, J. M. Cohen (London: Harvill Press, 1962), pp. 111 ff.

31. Robert M. Stein, *Incest and Human Love* (Baltimore: Penguin Books, 1974), p. 119.

32. James Hillman, *The Myth of Analysis* (Evanston: Northwestern University Press, 1972), pp. 280 ff.

33. Ibid., p. 297. See also the novels of Doris Lessing, particularly *The Four-Gated City* in which the heroine Martha Quest culminates her personal, spiritual, and psychological journey in achieving an androgynous consciousness. See also Caroline G. Heilbrun, *Towards Androgyny*.

34. O'Neill, *Open Marriage*, p. 146.

Chapter 7

1. Margaret Mead, *Male and Female: A Study of the Sexes in a Changing World* (New York: Dell Publishing Co., 1949), p. 188.

2. Arthur and Libby Colman, *Pregnancy: The Psychological Experience* (New York: Herder and Herder, 1971), pp. 25–26. See also p. 61 describing loss of control in labor.

3. Ibid., p. 24.

4. Ibid., p. 1.

5. Ibid., p. 28.

6. Ibid., pp. 13–14.

7. James Frazer, *The Golden Bough*, 3d ed., vol. 3, part 2 (London: MacMillan and Co., 1922), pp. 148 ff.

8. H. A. Hays, *The Dangerous Sex: The Myth of Feminine Evil* (New York: Pocket Books, 1964) proposes the thesis that female sexuality was seen as deviant and was hated and feared by men and that taboos were created to protect male phallic power from the debilitating effect of women.

9. Frazer, *Golden Bough*, p. 156. "Thus, among the Greek Indians a lad at initiation has to abstain for 12 moons from picking his ears or scratching his head with his fingers; he had to use small a stick for these purposes."

10. Ibid., p. 149.

11. Audrey I. Richards, *Chisungu: A Girl's Initiation Ceremony among the Bemba of Northern Rhodesia* (London: Faber and Faber, 1956), p. 124.

12. Ibid., pp. 183 ff.

13. M. Esther Harding, *Women's Mysteries: Ancient and Modern* (New York: G. P. Putman's Sons, 1971), p. 68.

14. Gordon Bourne, *Pregnancy* (London: Pan Books Ltd., 1975), p. 9.

15. Ibid., p. 10.

16. Ibid., p. 21.

17. Deborah Tanzer with Jean Libman Block, *Why Natural Childbirth?*

(Garden City: Doubleday and Co., 1972). Books such as these stress the positive elements of natural childbirth and the importance of developing a positive attitude in the father and mother to the experience through use of prophylactic methods. The general tone is overwhelmingly positive and tends to ignore the ambiguous or negative experiences and feelings.

18. Simone de Beauvoir, *The Second Sex*, trans. and ed. H. M. Parshley (New York: Alfred A. Knopf, 1952), pp. 466 ff.

19. Ibid., p. 468.

20. Ibid., p. 467, cf. p. 467.

21. M. Esther Harding, *The Way of All Women* (New York: G. P. Putnam's Sons, 1970), pp. 171 ff.

22. Ibid., p. 172.

23. Rollo May, *Love and Will* (New York: W. W. Norton and Co., 1969), p. 71, cf. pp. 66–71.

24. Colman, *Pregnancy: The Psychological Experience.*

25. Havelock Ellis, *Studies in the Psychology of sex*, vol. 2 (New York: Random House, 1936), p. 206.

26. Sheila Kitzinger, *The Experience of Childbirth* (New York: Taplinger Publishing Co., 1972), p. 84.

27. Germaine Greer, *The Female Eunuch* (St. Alban's: Granada Publishing Ltd., 1971), p. 96.

28. Mead, *Male and Female*, pp. 106, 166.

29. Harding, *Way of All Women*, p. 162.

30. Sheila Kitzinger, *Giving Birth: The Parents' Emotions in Childbirth* (New York: Taplinger Publishing Co., 1971), p. 43.

31. Therese Benedek, "The Psychobiology of Pregnancy," *Readings in the Psychology of Women*, ed. Judith M. Bardwick (New York: Harper and Row, 1972), p. 248.

32. Léon Chertok, *Motherhood and Personality* (London: Tavistock Publications Ltd., 1969), pp. 30–32.

33. Julia A. Sherman, *On the Psychology of Women: A Survey of Empirical Studies* (Springfield: Charles C. Thomas, 1971), pp. 194 ff.

34. A. A. Baker, *Psychiatric Disorders in Obstetrics* (Oxford: Blackwell Scientific Publications, 1967), p. 34.

35. Léon Chertok, "The Psychopathology of Vomiting in Pregnancy," *Modern Perspectives in Psycho-Obstetrics*, ed. John G. Howells (New York: Brunner/Mazel Publishers, 1972), p. 271.

36. G. L. Bibring, *Psychoanal. Stud. Child* 14:113, 1959, referred to by Kent Kyger and Warren W. Webb in "Progesterone Levels and Psychological State in Normal Women," *American Journal of Obstetrics and Gynecology*, 15, July 1972, p. 759.

37. Colman, *Pregnancy*, p. 10; cf. p. 7.

38. Ibid., p. 32.

39. Ibid., p. 48.

40. Ibid., p. 64; cf. p. 48.

41. Kitzinger, *Experience of Childbirth*, p. 23.

42. Ibid., p. 148.

43. Suzanne Parenteau-Carreau, *Love and Life*, trans. and adapt. Arthur W. Johnson (Ottawa: Serena, 1974), p. 20.

44. Tanzer and Block, *Why Natural Childbirth?* pp. 166 ff.

45. Kitzinger, *Giving Birth*, p. 38.

46. Sydney Brandon, "Psychiatric Illiness in Women," *Nursing Mirror*, 21 January 1972, p. 18.

Chapter 8

1. Angela Barron McBride, *The Growth and Development of Mothers* (New York: Harper and Row, 1973), p. 33.

2. See *The Womanly Art of Breast-feeding* (Franklin Park: La Leche League International, 1963), p. 32.

3. Erich Neumann, *The Great Mother*, trans. Ralph Manheim (Princeton: Princeton University Press, 1963), p. 32.

4. See *The Womanly Art of Breast-feeding*, p. 7.

5. Mary Daly, *The Church and the Second Sex* (New York: Harper and Row, 1968), p. 149.

6. Haim G. Ginott, *Between Parent and Child: New Solutions to Old Problems* (New York: Macmillan Co., 1965), p. 167.

7. McBride, *Growth and Development of Mothers*, p. 127.

8. Erich Fromm, *The Art of Loving* (New York: Bantam Books, 1963), p. 55.

9. Alexander Lowen, "The Spiral of Growth: Love, Sex, and Pleasure," *Love Today*, ed. Herbert A. Otto (New York: Dell Publishing Co., 1972), p. 22.

10. McBride, *Growth and Development of Mothers*, p. 117.

11. Elizabeth Janeway, *Man's World, Woman's Place* (New York: William Morrow and Co., 1971), p. 196.

12. McBride, *Growth and Development of Mothers*, p. 11.

13. Joyce Brothers, *Woman* (New York: McFadden-Bartell, 1961), pp. 113–14, 117, as quoted in McBride, *Growth and Development of Mothers*, p. 10.

14. Irene Claremont de Castillejo, *Knowing Woman: A Feminine Psychology* (New York: Harper and Row, 1973), p. 121.

15. Neumann, *Great Mother*, p. 189.

16. See McBride, *Growth and Development of Mothers*, pp. 128 ff.

17. A. A. Baker, *Psychiatric Disorders in Obstetrics* (Oxford: Blackwell Scientific Publications, 1967), p. 105.

18. M. Esther Harding, *Women's Mysteries: Ancient and Modern* (New York: Bantam Books, 1971), pp. 226–42.

19. Ibid., pp. 228–29.

20. Ibid., p. 239.

21. Janeway, *Man's World, Woman's Place*, p. 162.

22. McBride, *Growth and Development of Mothers*, p. 57.

23. Judith M. Bardwick, ed., *Readings on the Psychology of Women* (New York: Harper and Row, 1972), p. 118.

24. Irene Claremont de Castillejo comments that "perhaps trust is all a woman can safely give her children" if love is to stay. See *Knowing Woman*, p. 121.

25. Ibid., p. 123.

Chapter 9

1. Mary Wollstonccraft, *A Vindication of the Rights of Women* (New York: W. W. Norton, 1967), p. 36.

2. George and Nena O'Neill, *Shifting Gears* (New York: Avon, 1975). Discusses how to handle the changes that often occur in the middle years as identity is redefined.

3. See Howard J. Tatum, "Current Concepts of Hormonal Treatment of the Menopause," *Proceedings of the Third Asia and Oceania Endocrine Congress, Manila Philippines*, January 2–6, 1967.

4. Ibid., p. 54.

5. *The Change of Life* (Montreal: Ayerst Laboratories, Division of Ayerts, McKenna and Harison Ltd.), pp. 7, 12.

6. Actuarial tables quoted by Howard Tatum suggest that the average life expectancy for women in 1900 was 38 years. It is now 78 years.

7. Margaret Mead, *Male and Female: A Study of the Sexes in a Chang-World* (New York: Dell Publishing Co., 1949) suggests that women after menopause were treated like men in many societies; they were no longer potentially harmful to men (pp. 229, 187).

8. Simone de Beauvoir, *The Second Sex*, trans. and ed. H. M. Parshley (New York: Alfred A. Knopf, 1952) comments that though menopause frees a woman from a patriarchally imposed slavery she is immediately put into "retirement" (p. 550).

9. "Menopause and Estrogen Therapy," a roundtable discussion in *Journal of Reproductive Medicine*, vol. 11, no. 6, December 1973, p. 235.

10. See Clara Thompson's discussion of the psychological aspects of the change of life in "Middle Age," reprinted in *Women Body & Culture*, ed. Signe Hammer (New York: Harper and Row), pp. 223–34.

11. C. G. Jung, "The Stages of Life," *Collected Works*, 1975.

12. De Beauvoir, *The Second Sex*, noted the turn to religion common to women in their search for a new life—in illusion and fantasy (pp. 546–57).

13. Irene Claremont de Castillejo, *Knowing Woman: A Feminine Psychology* (New York: Harper and Row, 1973), p. 146.

14. Ibid., p. 161.

Chapter 10

1. The behavioristic studies support Erik Erikson's thesis that the possibility for personal development in old age is based on fulfillment of the stages of early adulthood. See Joseph Kuypers, "Ego Functioning in Old Age: Early Adult Life Antecedents," *Journal of Aging and Human Development*, vol. 5, no. 2, 1974, p. 157.

2. I am indebted to an excellent article by Myrna I. Lewis and Robert N. Butler, "Why Is Women's Lib Ignoring Old Women?" *Journal of Aging and Human Development*, vol. 3, 1972, p. 223.

3. This was reported in an article entitled "Accelerated Aging and the T.V. Commercial" by J. Scott Francher in *Journal of Aging and Human Development*, vol. 4, no. 3, 1973, p. 245.

4. See Jerome Ellison, *The Last Third of Life Club* (Philadelphia: Pilgrim Press, 1973).

5. Erik Erikson describes this stage of integrity or despair in *Identity: Youth and Crisis* (New York: W. W. Norton, 1968), pp. 139–40.

6. The term *life-reviewing* is used by psychologists of aging. It has been found to be an essential psychological process in old age if a final sense of identity is to be reached. See R. N. Butler, "The Life-Review: An Interpretation of Reminiscence in the Aged," *Psychiatry*, vol. 26, 1963, pp. 65–76.

7. See Irene de Castillejo, *Knowing Woman: A Feminine Psychology* (New York: Harper and Row, 1973).

8. Renaldo Maduro, "Artistic Creativity and Aging in India," *Journal of Aging and Human Development*, vol. 5, no. 4, 1974. This fascinating article suggests that artistic creativity *increases* with age in this Hindu community of painters. It is accepted that old age is a time to engage in an arduous process of self-exploration and scanning of inner resources. This attention to inner creativity involves an element of withdrawal from social interaction in this process of self-transformation through creative expression (p. 303).

9. Lewis and Butler, "Why Is Women's Lib Ignoring Old Women?" This article points out that 65 percent of all older women are on their own.

10. Ibid., p. 227.

11. Robert E. Kavanaugh, *Facing Death* (Baltimore: Penguin Books, 1972) stresses the need for allowing grief to have its own time.

12. See C. G. Jung, "The Stages of Life," *The Portable Jung*, ed. Joseph Campbell (New York: Viking Press, 1971), p. 20.

13. Elizabeth Kubler-Ross, *Death: The Final Stage of Growth* (Englewood Cliffs: Prentice Hall, 1975). The final section entitled "Omega"

advocates our need to find a sense of history, to know that we are part of what has come before and what is yet to come, in order to reach peace in our dying (p. 167).

14. Joseph Kuypers, "Ego Functioning in Old Age," shows that the fulfillment of an individual's intellectual capacities in early life has a significant impact on the ability to develop in old age.

15. See Paul Tillich, *The Courage to Be* (New Haven: Yale University Press, 1952).

16. Hermann Feifel, "Death—Relevant Variable in Psychology," *Existential Psychology*, ed. Rollo May (New York: Random House, 1960), p. 68.

INDEX OF PROPER NAMES

INDEX OF SUBJECTS